LIVING THE WHEEL

11/1/9?

Dear Gloria
Thanks for the
beauty convoy
Love
Annabelle

LIVING⛓THE⛓WHEEL

Working with Emotion, Terror, and Bliss through Imagery

Annabelle Nelson

SAMUEL WEISER, INC.

York Beach, Maine

First published in 1993 by
Samuel Weiser, Inc.
Box 612
York Beach, ME 03910

Library of Congress Cataloging-in-Publication Data

Nelson, Annabelle.
    Living the wheel : working with emotion, terror, and bliss through
    imagery / by Annabelle Nelson.
        p.   cm.
    Includes bibliographical references and index.
    1. Spiritual life.   2. Visualization   3. Imagery (Psychology)
4. Subconsciousness. 5. Emotions—Religious aspects. 6. Dualism
(Religion)—Controversial literature.   I. Title
    BL624.N44   1993
    291.4′4--dc20   93-16810
                                                                CIP

ISBN 0-87728-782-1
MG

Cover art is from a painting titled "Ancient Memories" by Rob Schouten.
Copyright © 1993 Rob Schouten. Used by kind permission of the artist.

Illustrations on text pages 1, 19, 37, 57, 85, 103, and 119 are copyright ©
1993 Cody Lundin. Used by kind permission.

Typeset in 11 point Palatino

Printed in the United States of America
99 98 97 96 95 94 93
10 9 8 7 6 5 4 3 2 1

The paper used in this publication meets the minimum requirements of
the American National Standard for Permanence of Paper for Printed
Library Materials Z39.48-1984.

To Bob, Jody, and McCoy

Table of Contents

Acknowledgments ix

Introduction xi

Chapter 1: Beyond Dualism 1

Chapter 2: Intuition 19

Chapter 3: Imagery 37

Chapter 4: Emotions 57

Chapter 5: Psychic Stuff 85

Chapter 6: Terrors and Demons 103

Chapter 7: Bliss and Peace 119

Afterword: Relationships 127

Appendix A: Who's Who 131

Appendix B: Imagery Readings 137

Appendix C: Imagery and Brain Physiology 141

Appendix D: Imagery Scripts 153

Bibliography 175

Index 181

About the Author 187

Acknowledgments

I would first like to honor and celebrate my many spiritual teachers. These include my mother, Jesus, B.K.S. Iyengar, Ram Dass, Lilias, Robert Burford, Buckminster Fuller, Saint John, Deva Lama, McCoy and Jody, Bob Hoffa, and the Buddha. A very special thanks and reverence to Shiva[1] who appeared to me and told me to write this book. The book is a humble offering to this experience. Linda Clark, the editorial assistant, is one of the most beautiful people I know. She gives in service over and over. Psychologists who have influenced my work in imagery deserve accolades. These are Jeanne Achterberg, Geir Kaufmann, and David Marks. Thanks also to editors who include Dee Gray, Joanie Maerzke, Mary Grace Lentz, Bev Santo, and Bob Hoffa. I would particularly like to thank the Earth my mother and the Sky my father for my walk in this dream world. Thanks also to the Indian people I have worked with over the last year for showing me gentleness and acceptance.

Some information in Chapter One is based on Native American concepts. I would like to ask forgiveness in advance if anything is misrepresented or used inappropriately. The intent is not to steal from them, but to use certain con-

---

[1]M. and J. Stutley in Dictionary of Hinduism (1977) state that Shiva is translated as auspicious and is the name applied to the storm-god Rudra. Shiva represents "supra-ethical and supra-personal dynamic evolution" (Stutley, 1977, p. 279). The word supra-ethical seems particularly appropriate for the theme of this book, since the attitudes and imagery techniques help a person move beyond the value judgments of the conscious mind to merge with the spirit self.

cepts to balance Western notions of reality. I would like to thank Will Numkena of the Hopi Tribe for concepts in the Four Direction story and information about the migrations. I would also like to thank Bernard Siquieros and Diane Jose, both of the Tohono O'odham Tribe for information about the Tohono O'odham maze. In addition I would like to thank David Begay of the Diné Tribe for information on the Dine Philosophy of Learning.

Introduction

During the 1960s, Alan Watts taught Zen philosophy in San Francisco. At the same time Timothy Leary and Richard Alpert took acid at Harvard to open Aldous Huxley's door of perception. People living in the U.S. pursued the spiritual dimension of life, to counterbalance the religion of science that had come to reign. The post-war U.S. society of the 1950s had believed that science and technology could solve all problems. But this left a dispirited culture; the mental and physical elements of life were celebrated, but the emotional and spiritual elements were denied. That which is suppressed gains momentum and energy. And the young people of the 1960s swarmed to experience the spirit in their lives through drugs and spiritual practices that would extend consciousness to transcendence. God was not science; rather it was the experience of bliss and interconnectedness to the lifeforce that prevaded all things.

Over the last 25 years, people have pursued meditation and yoga, paths primarily from Asia, to rediscover the spiritual dimension of the human experience. This energy has created space within our culture for people to popularize and commercialize the states of spiritual awareness that include psychic perception and altered states of awareness. At this point, the U.S. culture seems to be at a juncture. How do we move concepts of spiritual development more into the cultural mainstream, while retaining their integrity? And how do people pursuing the spiritual path move to the next stage of awareness? This stage insists on emotional healing and

xii ○ Annabelle Nelson

the transcendence of dualism about what is true and not true about spiritual growth.

We now need methods and frames for spiritual development that fit the North American experience and which resonate with the culture and the landscape. We also need honesty about what can be expected on the spiritual path.

This book is about the use of imagery to open the unconscious mind to contact the spirit self hidden there. Imagery techniques give tools and knowledge to continue the spiritual journey after the initial "highs" that result from adopting a spiritual practice become interspersed with disturbing emotions and visions.

Through spiritual practice, a person develops a discipline of attention by learning to focus on the breath, body movement, or rhythm. This focus serves to open the doors to the unconscious mind, which holds suppressed trauma and karma. It is important to open the unconscious and clean out this debris, because buried underneath the debris is the gem of the person's spirit. The goal is to unite with this spirit over time.

Living the Wheel presents psychological and physiological perspectives on the process of imagery. *Imagery* used here means thinking in internal sensations, such as sound, taste, vision, movement, touch or smell, without external input. The thinking process of imagery is unique since it can travel in the unconscious mind at will. Thinking in images also requires an internal focus of attention, learning the same skills derived through spiritual practice. As such, imagery can become a stabilizing tool for emotional health to fuel the spiritual path. Imagery, as studied in cognitive psychology, neuropsychology, and shamanism is consistent with the scientific culture of the U.S., as well as the Native North American spiritual roots in the land.

The first half of the book begins slowly with introductory information on intuition and the existence of subtle realities beyond time and space. A discussion of humanistic psychology, Hindu philosophy, and neuropsychology creates the conceptual framework for altered state experiences in multiple realities.

The second half of the book jumps into the abyss of spiritual experience. The stages of emotional disintegration that accompany spiritual development are explained, along with attitudes and imagery practices that assist the collapse of the conscious mind. Even though the process is healing, emergence from the unconscious can create disturbing and disintegrative emotions and visions. This can be very shattering. The healing of emotional trauma is essential at this stage. A person must move out of psychological denial to fully integrate with the spirit.

Shamanism is included in the book as a model for working with the dark forces that emerge from the unconscious. Darkness and death are necessary components for healing the individual. Joseph Campbell's metaphors of the hero-heroine's journey are also used to explain the need for facing the depths inside the being. When the hero-heroine metaphor is used for the journey into the darkness within the self, then the outcome can be a uniting with the power of the spirit connected to the universe.

Living the Wheel is above all a practical text with guidelines for learning to sharpen the intuition, to work with disintegrative emotional states, to create more vivid imagery within the mind, to use psychic information from channelers or oracles, and to heighten psychic perception. Imagery exercises at the end of each chapter help readers practice techniques. Appendices contain guidelines for using imagery with other people, references to learn more about imagery, and notes on major figures in the psychospiritual movement.

Living the Wheel has a uniquely North American perspective. Most of the spiritual practices pursued by people in the United States are from Asia. Yoga, meditation, mandalas, breathing exercises, and Taoist attitudes help train attention and produce profound insights toward self-awareness. These practices are extremely helpful, but most contain a dimension that does not directly deal with the emotional side effects of spiritual development. Because Asian practices do not teach techniques to heal emotions, often denial of emotional issues results. This, in turn, can arrest progress in spiritual development. The North American human consciousness differs from the Asian consciousness. Native North Americans have kept shamanic practices alive that prescribe identifying with the Earth's energy instead of transcending the natural forces within the human body. Using these practices as a model, North Americans may respond better to spiritual paths that accept the human condition, including all emotions, in order to transform the emotions toward energy for the spiritual path.

Living the Wheel proposes imagery practices that heal and embrace human emotions. These can complement spiritual practices. Moving through our humanity—both our body and emotions—with the connection to the Mother Earth as our primary teacher can be an effective awakening path for North Americans.

— Annabelle Nelson

LIVING THE WHEEL

Chapter One

Beyond Dualism

Eons and eons and millennia and millennia ago, the land masses of the Earth were all one. There was one great continent, called Pangia and there was one great ocean that teemed with life. At that time the Earth was ruled by the four directions. The east or morning was a time for preparation. The south or noon was a time for activity. The west or evening was a time for reflection; and the north or night was a time for reverence.

The Creator had made four peoples for each of the four directions: red, yellow, white, and black. The Creator had given each of the peoples a special gift unique in and of itself. The peoples' charge was to move out into the four directions and to develop their unique gifts.

A meeting of all the peoples was scheduled every ten years at a great mesa in the middle of the continent to share these gifts. The Creator appointed coyote as the peace keeper. The coyote may seem an odd choice, since he is small and insignificant. But the coyote is a master of survival and can raise a racket with his howl. When the peoples fell into disharmony and quarreled, the coyote would howl and howl until they came back into harmony. When the peoples would gather at the great mesa, the coyote would stay in the mountains around the mesa to make sure that all was well.

Time passed and the peoples progressed in developing their gifts. Every ten years they would meet at the great mesa. There came a time at one gathering when a great quarrel broke out. The peoples began to gather and display their gifts, but an argument began on who had the best gift. The coyote began howling. But it was to no avail. The peoples would not stop quarreling. Finally, the Creator sent each of the peoples out to their own direction to begin their great migrations.

Millennia passed and, over time, Pangaea broke into continents. The great ocean was divided by the continents, and the peoples were separated. The peoples continued their migrations and continued developing their gifts. Over time and more millennia, things began to change.

Because of the changes people could travel from continent to continent, and could talk from continent to continent. At first when the people of the four directions saw each other, they were afraid because the differences between them were so great. But then a beautiful thing began to happen. Some peoples from each direction returned to the great mesa, which was now on North America. Even though afraid, they began to watch each other and learn from each other. More peoples were drawn to the great mesa. Together the peoples of the four directions began to put the gifts together to create the whole. And on that day they say that the coyote smiled.

Western Society Out of Balance

This story gives a metaphor of how to create a life in harmony and in balance. We might postulate that each of the gifts was a way to look at the world, or a reality, unique in and of itself. By learning to deal in each of these realities a person becomes whole or learns about the entire wheel of existence. When only one direction is elevated as the truth, then one's existence will be in disharmony.

The Hopi migration stories explain why the Western world view is out of balance. When the Creator sent the peoples of the world out on migrations, they were to follow the four cardinal directions of east, south, west and north. The peoples were instructed to begin in the east and then proceed in each of the directions in sequence. The east was the direction of preparation, which led to the direction of the south for learning how to make a living on the Earth. Then the peoples were to proceed to the west to learn reflection, thinking, and planning. The final direction, north, helped teach the peoples reverence and the mysteries that bind the spirit world with the material.

In the Native American wheel, each direction carries a certain energy or quality. Humans must pay attention to each direction's lesson and proceed with the directions in the order that they occur beginning in the east, to create a life of harmony and balance. However, the white people out of arrogance skipped the first two directions and went west first. Because of this the people of the Western world missed the lessons of the first two directions and now live out of balance.

The direction of the west deals with reflection, introspection, thinking, and planning. The Western world view is one that uses a scientific method of analysis and experimentation to explain and define reality. Through the refinement of these thought forms, the West created the scientific revolution. As a result of this method, great achievements have been realized with technology. However, the West, by emphasizing only one direction, has created a people who live in disharmony and a society that is out of balance.

Western society has created a view of reality in which there is a correct way as defined by science. Other ways that don't conform to the scientific method become incorrect by default. This could be termed dualistic since events or perceptions are classified in two divisions. Reality becomes narrowed to the parameters that conform to scientific inquiry. All other phenomena that do not conform to this paradigm are simply not real.

The reality defined by this form of dualism requires that a large part of the human mind and experience be denied. That which is outside of science has no expression. The non-scientific elements of the self include the emotional, the intuitive and the symbolic. The linear, analytic mind is elevated to truth in Western society, and as a result a person becomes out of balance because other necessary attributes are not attended to.

The scientific model of reality has helped create sophisticated achievements, such as cars and satellites, but it has also served to remove humans from their true nature. Since science is conceptual it deals with ideas abstracted from nature. The abstract concept, such as the principle of gravity, is the underlying basis that explains natural phenomena. At times, though, the abstraction takes on a life of its own and loses its connection to reality. Science can create a nuclear reactor to produce electricity, but it cannot figure out what to do with nuclear waste which is carcinogenic for 250,000 years. The abstraction of science keeps humans away from their natural connection with the world, and creates a society out of balance.

The lack of balance in the individual is reflected in society. The U.S. society is on the verge of breaking apart with devastating problems that seem to have no solution. Inner city violence, crack, out-of-control health care costs, and one-fifth of all children living in poverty are just a few of this society's problems.

Mystical realities are assumed to be false, because they do not follow the rules of science. Dualism, in part, is necessary to the scientific model. Things need to be proved to be correct or incorrect. However this dualism has grown out of control. It has taken over all types of thinking in Western culture.

Emphasizing the West, in and of itself, is not "wrong" or bad. If we branded the direction west as the problem, we would be creating a new dualism. Each direction has a special energy and is necessary to create the whole. The task is not to abandon science or analytic thought, but to have it take its proper place in relationship to other realities.

Dualism and the Mind

The mind is complex and holds many types of thought forms. Only a very small part of the mind thinks in abstract analysis. Therefore dualism supports the use of a small part of the mind and denies the rest of the mind's function.

The conscious mind, or the thoughts that run through a person's head, serves to create a stable reality. Young children receive training from their culture that helps build the structure of the conscious mind. Since Western society uses the scientific model to define reality, the conscious mind becomes equated with linear thinking. All other parts of the mind that think in a different manner are relegated to the unconscious.

Other thought forms become "unreal" and are not supported by the cultural view of what is accepted as reality. Thought forms outside the scientific model are non-linear and have two basic qualities in common. The first quality is that they are simultaneous in nature. This means that a lot of different information is taken in at once. Information is not put in order and processed one piece at a time. The second quality of non-linear thinking is that it cannot be analyzed. Its meaning is not logically apparent.

Intuitive thought forms have both of these qualities. A person gets a "sense" of something from taking in a lot of information at once. The person seems to know something, but cannot say how he or she came about this information. Emotional information is also simultaneous in nature. Feelings do not come in a sequence, and people often do not know why they are feeling a certain way. Symbolic thinking, where people see images or forms in their minds, cannot be processed in a sequence, since the whole symbol or image is taken in at once. Symbols also cannot be analyzed in a specific linear way.

Society allows artists or geniuses to think in these ways, because they are outside of the mainstream culture. They do not necessarily have to deal with what is defined as the "real world." For most people however, expressing thoughts that are outside of the logical, abstract mode results in their being labeled as ignorant or even as insane. These people are seen as being out of touch with reality.

The scientific dualism of our culture reinforces psychological dualism. Defense mechanisms in the mind push events into the unconscious if they seem dangerous. Dangerous thoughts or perceptions are those that would disturb the individual's internal stability. In the current cultural collective view of reality, it is dangerous to admit that certain phenomena are real. For example, a person may know something right before it happens or dream the event the night before. This person thinks that he or she is crazy because a reality that supposedly does not exist is taking hold.

Scientific reality examines causes and effects of phenomena and therefore looks at time in a linear manner. One event occurs after another. If time is a line, then one cannot know things before they happen. But if time were a circle, there may be a dimension in the middle where time comes and goes in waves.

The dualistic view of reality carried to its extreme implies that there is only one correct way to think, and many incorrect ways. But this, in itself, is dangerous because dualism acts to suppress the potential of the mind by limiting the definition of thinking to be conscious awareness. A non-dualistic model of reality contains the concept that there are many modes of thinking and many realities.

The Unconscious: Savage or Wise

From a psychological perspective, dualism results in the conscious mind becoming correct or real, and the unconscious mind becoming incorrect and out of touch with reality. Another way this can be phrased is that the conscious mind is civilized and the unconscious mind is primitive.

In the Western view, the unconscious mind must be controlled because if it is opened that which is outside civilization may be exposed. A person may return to his or her animal nature, which may not be rational. The conscious mind thus takes on the role of using logic and reasoning to overcome and suppress the unconscious mind. An individual tames the self by attempting to deny the existence of the unconscious mind in an attempt to conform to the expectations of society. But the problem is that by giving the control to the conscious mind, the person loses the connection with the parts of the self that are creative, healing, and connected to nature. The person strives to become almost inhuman, by controlling and denying the natural parts of the self. In effect, a person becomes what he or she is not.

To become whole, it is important to open oneself to the forces that have been sealed into the unconscious mind. The serpent is a good metaphor for what resides in the unconscious mind. The serpent represents the knowledge of the ancient mysteries of creation locked in the formation of the Earth. The serpent also represents the cycle of life and rebirth, since it metaphorically dies as it sheds its skin and is reborn as it grows a new skin. It is interesting what cultures hold the serpent in respect and what cultures vilify it. In some

Native American tribes, the serpent is revered as it is in China, since it symbolizes the mysterious knowledge of life, death, and creation. In the Western culture, the serpent is equated with Adam and Eve's fall from grace, and therefore symbolizes evil. The serpent must be killed, just as the darkness of the unconscious mind must be suppressed and avoided.

But the unconscious mind holds many benefits for the individual. It holds what the Hindus call the *atman* or the spirit self, which is connected to the life force that pervades all things. It also holds what humanistic psychology calls the actualizing tendency or the unconscious force that creates healing and self-fulfillment. Scientists and artists rely on insights from the unconscious for creativity. They do not figure out discoveries and new expressions; rather they wait for the insight to emerge from the unconscious.

In today's society there are glimpses that the unconscious mind needs to be delved into and integrated into a person's awareness. It is becoming clearer that it is a fallacy to attempt to stamp out and civilize what is dark and primitive in the unconscious. By doing this, one in essence commits suicide. The healing, spiritual, and creative potential of the person is denied.

What is ancient is not necessarily primitive; it may be wise. For example the ethnobotany of indigenous people provides the basis for most of modern medicine's pharmaceuticals. Also, the rituals, songs, and vision quests of indigenous people that were used to stay in tune with the natural and spirit worlds form the basis for current therapy and personal growth workshops.

Elements of U.S. society are rediscovering that ancient ways buried in humankind's collective unconscious can form the basis for healing and returning our lives to balance with the natural world. Through the unconscious a person gains access to parts of the self that have been previously denied or suppressed. Attributes of the self in the unconscious are healing in nature and can assist a person on the quest for wholeness.

By becoming ancient and new at the same time, people can learn to move into multiple realities and merge with the spirit self in the unconscious.

The Middle Brain

The linear, conscious mind of the scientific society is sometimes equated with the cerebral cortex of the brain. This is the gray matter full of wrinkles. The cortex is vitally important because it contains higher order thinking skills like planning, organizing, reasoning, and deducting.

The dualism in science makes the cortex important and the older (in terms of evolution of the human species) and more primitive parts of the brain less important. For example, most researchers in neurophysiology examine the cortex and term other parts of the brain as paleomammalian or reptilian. However, it may be that just as the primitive unconscious holds wisdom for today, other parts of the brain hold wisdom as well. The dualism in the scientific model makes the newer part of the brain, the cortex, important. The older structures of the brain are ignored.

Some Native North American Indian teachers are pointing out that there are older parts of the brain that are critical in helping people learn to live in balance. Dhyani Ywahoo,[1] a holder of the priestcraft tradition of the Tsalgi tribe (Cherokee), claims that there is a middle brain underneath the cerebral cortex. This middle brain, according to Ywahoo, is responsible for balancing the whole being.

There is physiological support for Ywahoo's contention. There is a structure in the middle of the brain which is called the limbic system. *Limbic* means rim in Latin. This rim-like structure that threads underneath the cortex is central in regu-

---

[1] Ywahoo, D. *Voices of Our Ancestors* (Denver, CO: Shambhala, 1987).

lating emotions, mediating intuition, creating altered states of consciousness, and communicating to the immune system. Large concentrations of neurotransmitters, such as endorphins and dopamine, are also found near the limbic system. These transmitters are implicated in states of arousal and bliss and are involved in addictive behaviors. Because of the significance of these functions this part of the brain seems very important for creating balance. It is interesting that the functions of the limbic system are non-linear. It may be important, because of our scientific model, for us to ignore or make these functions unimportant, because if we admitted that they existed, we might have to change our definition of reality. Opening to the middle brain and recognizing its importance may create an avenue for us to move beyond dualism.

Beyond Dualism: The Wheel Metaphor

The scientific model of reality has its role and makes significant contributions to society. The problem is that it has become tyrannical and created a societal and psychological dualism that relegates other realities to the realm of the unreal, dark, primitive, crazy, or ignorant. It is hard to move beyond dualism because there is an inherent assumption in this paradigm that one way is correct. By using the thought forms prescribed by the scientific model one can never escape the model. Many writers in the spiritual movement in the U.S. attempt to use the conscious mind to figure out how to move into the unconscious. The conscious mind will protect itself and its current state of stability and not allow the person to move beyond its limit. To move beyond the scientific paradigm, people need models to help them experience other thought forms, particularly intuitive ones, without analyzing them.

Rediscovering an ancient model of reality may teach people techniques for balance. The circle or the wheel provides such a model. It is important to point out that the task is not to find the *one* other reality that the scientific model has obscured or suppressed. That would continue the dualistic paradigm in another form. For example, the right brain/left brain model would say that the scientific model is akin to the left brain, and to become more integrated and balanced, people need to add right hemispheric activity. But there are many ways of knowing and thinking about reality. It is not a matter of teaching people the one other reality; it is rather a matter of teaching people to experience multiple realities. The wheel model gives a method of tolerating multiple realities and imbuing each with equal importance. The following sections describe three wheel models from Native American traditions.

The O'odham Maze

The Tohono O'odham tribe lives in the Sonoran desert amidst saguaro cactus and palo verde trees. The name Tohono O'odham, means desert people. Rising from the desert is Wawgiwulka, a huge and majestic mountain. The O'odham creator, I'itoi, lived high on the mountain in a cave when he was on Earth. The symbol of I'itoi and the mountain is a maze. The maze represents life; when one is born he or she starts at the opening of the maze and the goal in life is to reach the inner peace at the middle of the maze. People make many wrong turns on the path, but there is always the chance to turn again and take a new route to the center.

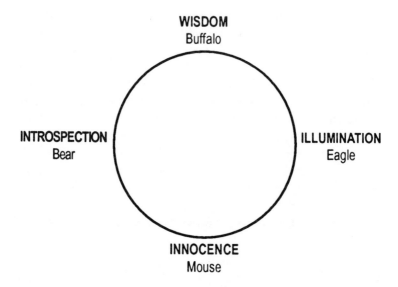

Figure 1. The Plains Medicine Wheel. Adapted from H. Storm's *Seven Arrows*.

The O'odham symbology of the spiritual path in life is non-linear. One moves through the maze of life without seeing the end with the mystery of creation residing all around one. A turn to a blocked part of the maze is not wrong in the dualistic sense, but an opportunity to redefine the route.

The Plains Wheel

The Plains Medicine Wheel (see figure 1) is documented in Storm's book *Seven Arrows*.[2] In this model of reality each cardinal direction of the Earth has a different energy, which is symbolized by a word and the metaphor of an animal. The wheel can be used as a method for creating a life in balance

---

[2] Storm, H. *Seven Arrows* (New York: HarperCollins, 1987).

and harmony. For example, a person could be born with an introspective personality. That person's job becomes the task of cultivating the energy of the other directions in the self. This can be done by spending time with people who have the other qualities or by creating ceremonies and rituals that embody the qualities of each of the directions. Other medicine wheels are subdivided into eighths or sixteenths. A life lived in harmony with creation is one marked by balancing the energies of the four directions.

It is a very important quality of the medicine wheel that no one direction is correct. All are equal to each other; each is necessary for the whole. This is a very different model of reality from scientific dualism, since there is not one correct reality nor one correct way of being. There is room around the circle for many different modes of knowing. The wheel mode for organizing reality allows the Native American world view to tolerate diversity and allows the spirit worlds to breathe in and out of everyday life.

The Diné Wheel

The Diné wheel is described by Herbert Benally.[3] *Diné* is the traditional name of the Navajo tribe and means the people. The Diné story of creation is used to create the wheel in figure 2 (on p. 14). In the origins of the Earth, the four directions played a fundamental role in creation. Each direction held a different quality, and together the directions could serve to balance life and human activity. When one lives in harmony with the directions, one has aligned the self with the forces of creation. The Diné wheel and story contains a beautiful metaphor for reclaiming an integrated human life rooted in the ancient mysteries of the Earth's creation.

---

[3] Benally, H. "Diné Philosophy of Learning." *Journal of Navajo Education* 6, 9-13.

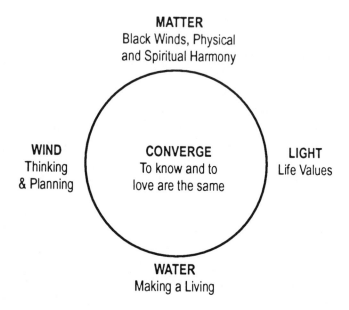

MATTER
Black Winds, Physical
and Spiritual Harmony

WIND
Thinking
& Planning

CONVERGE
To know and to
love are the same

LIGHT
Life Values

WATER
Making a Living

Figure 2. The Diné Wheel. Adapted from H. Benally's 1988 article "Diné Philosophy of Learning" in *Journal of Navajo Education* 6: 9-13.

Navajo Community College, under the direction of David Begay, is using the Diné wheel to create a balanced curriculum, demonstrating that the wheel metaphor has practical significance and relevance to modern daily life. It can return lives to balance even today.

In Navajo ceremonies, the east is the beginning and the directions are addressed in sequence in the proper order. Possibly, individuals outside of Navajo society could use the wheel concept to address the energies of the Earth beyond the scientific dualistic construct. By aligning with the four directions of the Earth, one is in proper relation to the Earth, which brings one in proper relation to the sun, which brings one in proper relation to the Universe, which brings one in proper relationship to all of creation.

Metaphoric Thinking

It is of absolute importance to stress that the thinking skills of the scientific model cannot be used by us to move out of that definition of reality. One cannot figure out or analyze the unconscious, because the unconscious is many different realities and is not necessarily logical. One has to give up the conscious mind's hold on reality to experience other realities. This takes retraining the mind to move beyond dualism.

It is not possible to use the scientific model to chart the unconscious mind and the subtle realities that exist there. The conscious mind exists to keep the person's awareness outside of the perceived dangers in the unconscious. Forces deep in the unconscious create the conscious mind. Therefore the conscious mind is the created, and the unconscious mind the creator. The created has a hard time explaining the creator. It is necessary to give up trying to know and analyzing in order to open to the unconscious.

Linear thinking is not capable of opening the unconscious mind. Another type of thought form needs to be developed. Earlier in the chapter, intuition was mentioned, as was symbolic thinking. Another term to describe intuitive or symbolic processing is metaphoric thinking. Metaphors resemble what is to be communicated, but they cannot be literally translated. When one thinks metaphorically, the information is allowed in and one perceives the truth of what is being presented. It is a matter of clarifying the perception so that the metaphor can move into the deep structure of the mind in the unconscious. The force in the unconscious then recognizes the metaphor.

The move to a circle, to tolerating multiple realities takes a belief that there is a part of the mind that will recognize the truth or the many truths even though one's conscious mind is not in control. This is very difficult for many people because they equate themselves with their conscious mind. It takes the willingness to let the mind be out of control, so the spirit self in the unconscious can be contacted.

Learning to tolerate paradoxes is also a necessary step. In paradoxical thinking one tolerates opposites in the mind simultaneously. In a paradox, contradictions are true. For example, in order to be strong one has to experience weakness. Paradoxes defy the scientific paradigm because they appear to be illogical. Therefore, working with paradoxes is a ripe avenue for teaching the conscious mind to tolerate multiple realities.

By relaxing the conscious mind's hold on reality, a person becomes aware of circles, learns to tolerate paradoxes, and realizes that no one way need exclude others in order to be true. The linear, analytic part of the mind still functions, but it does not deny or control the other parts of the mind. A person develops cognitive flexibility and resiliency. In time, as the conscious mind releases its hold, the person will start to experience the subtle realms of reality that underlie the material level. These are the spirit and psychic worlds. It is difficult to transform the mind. However, the rewards are great for embarking on this journey. Through this process one finds the spirit self that is transcendent and connected to all other spirits. The spirit self gives nourishment and guidance on the path to the eternal.

The remainder of this book is designed to help a person move out of the conscious mind and tolerate multiple realities. Fine-tuning the intuition is necessary, because the intuition will give a person a way to judge what is happening in multiple realities. If realities are charted that do not follow the rule of linear analysis, then a person will need help in understanding what is going on, how to integrate perceptions, and how to take action if necessary. Learning to think in images is helpful in collapsing the conscious mind. Imagery is the primitive language of the body, and it can affect immune activity, induce deep relaxation, and create ecstatic visions for spiritual guidance. People also need to learn how to heal emotional issues since suppressed emotional trauma can cloud psychic and intuitive perception. Finally, people need some parameters and ideas about what lies ahead when they give up the firm linear reality.

It has always been the right time for people to live a life in balance and harmony. One can hope that now is the time when people will actually integrate the parts of themselves that are necessary for a balanced life. As individuals make these changes in their inner worlds, shifts in the outer world will follow. Healthy integrated people will help move a society and the planet towards health. This is important and necessary work.

Imagery Exercise: Aligning to the Earth

Have someone read the following exercise to you as you listen, or you or someone else can dictate this on a tape for later use. Make sure whoever is reading talks slowly. When listening to the instructions sit or lie comfortably. Keep your eyes open or closed. Take any position that feels comfortable to you. It is good to play music that makes you feel calm during the entire imagery exercise.

Imagine that you are outside in one of your favorite places. You have been to this setting before. You felt happy and calm the last time you were here. You are alone today, but not lonely. There is no place you have to go and nothing that you have to do. Things will wait so you don't need to think about them now.

You start noticing the world of nature around you. Is there a breeze on your cheek? What color is the sky? Are there clouds? How do your feet feel as you pick each one up and move it? How do your feet feel as they contact the ground? Notice the colors of green. Feel a branch scratch your arm as you walk by. Notice sounds and movements.

Notice the texture of the ground around you. Try to bond with the scene so strongly that you get the impression that your senses are eating or consuming what they perceive.

You walk around a bit in the setting and after a time you find a place where you would like to sit or lie down to rest. As you move to the ground, you start to sense vividly the ground where you are sitting or lying: the colors, textures, sizes, and shapes. You pick some dirt up in your hands and smell it and feel it. Imagine that you are moving into the Earth below you, almost as an ant would. It is as if you are moving down into the ground. You feel connected and a part of the Earth. You have a very strong sensation that your body is made out of the same composition as the Earth. Take your time to feel this sensation fully.

After a time, you move your attention to the sky. You notice the blue of the sky, and as you breathe in, it is almost as if you are taking the sky into your lungs. As you become fixated on the sky above you, you take in more and more breaths. Soon you feel very light. It is as if you can move up into the sky with each breath. You are light and moving upward. Your movement accelerates, and you speed up into the air through the atmosphere out into the indigo violet of dark space. Magically you can still breathe. Take your time to feel the sensation of moving out into space.

At a certain point, you turn around in your journey and you look back at the Earth. You notice its beauty and the details of the land masses and clouds. You notice the Earth's colors and textures from space. You realize that this is your home and you feel connected and full of love for the Earth. Stay with that feeling and the view of the Earth as long as possible.

After you are done looking, you move back to your place on the Earth and feel rested and refreshed. Before you leave your site notice the sun's path and give thanks to the four directions—the east, south, west and north.

Chapter Two

Intuition

I am standing on a sandbar. It is not too big, but I see it extending, jutting out into the river. The sand bar is light-colored sand and moves out to a point in the river. The river is running well with new water from snows. Behind me are tepees with smoke coming out the tops. Many men, women, and children are sitting and working by the tepees. I am standing at the end of the sand bar and notice that a drum is beating. My feet are moving in a slow and rhythmic way. One foot strikes the earth as the drum beats, then the other with the next beat. There are now many people on the sand bar and our feet strike the ground together, slowly and firmly. The beat grows stronger. As our feet contact the ground, the beat moves through the Earth and reverberates. I hear a voice that joins the rhythm of our feet. "The wheel is turning. The wheel is turning." The drum, the voice, the feet grow stronger and take me over. "The wheel is turning."

What is Intuition?

To turn the wheel, or to unite with the deep purpose inside each of us, we must awaken to our intuitive voices. The deep power within is accessed by bringing our awareness to our intuition. This lets us become connected to the Earth beneath our feet.

Intuition is a deep knowing or sensing. It is almost like reaching out and feeling something in the dark, but not with our hands, with our minds. Blind people often sense a wall before they get to it. This is intuition. It is a type of perception, and it is the voice of the spirit deep inside of us.

The mind is quite a miracle. We have 100 trillion neural connections—more than the number of known stars in the universe. We are only aware of about thirty percent of our brain with our conscious mind. That means that a large part of our mind is unconscious and nonverbal in nature. Intuition operates from our unconscious mind. As we learn to be more intuitive, more of our unconscious mind becomes conscious. This creates an expanded awareness.

Intuition is Acausal

Intuition has unique qualities. It is difficult to explain these qualities, because intuition for the most part is nonverbal. Our rational mind communicates in words, but our intuitive mind communicates with a feeling, a picture, or a flash of insight. This makes it sometimes difficult to talk about intuition. It would be easier to draw pictures about it, but with some effort we can get a sense of it through words.

When you sense something intuitively you do not know if you caused the thought or if somebody else caused it. For example, you may think of your best friend Dee Dee, and in a few moments Dee Dee calls you. What happened? What was the time sequence? Did you cause Dee Dee to think of you? Or was Dee Dee thinking of you which prompted you to think of her? You do not know.

Since intuition is acausal, there is no time frame involved. Causality implies a time sequence—first this happens, then that. Often you can say the second event is caused by the first event, hence the word causal. But intuition does not conform to a time sequence.

The fact that intuition is acausal is quite a beautiful thing, because it prevents you from what new-agers call "egoing-out." "Egoing-out" is a feeling that you are a little god capable of powerful actions apart from the universal force. The main feeling during egoing-out is one of superiority to others. If you think that you are controlling and sending intuitive information, this may increase your sense of power over others and your feelings of superiority.

For those interested in working and living in expanded awareness, this is a major danger. A feeling of personal power separate from the spirit that intertwines all of us creates separation and ultimately suffering. From a Christian sense, you are setting yourself above God. From a Hindu sense, you are creating new karma. And from a psychological framework, you are creating a false sense of ego by thinking that you are superior.

Thinking that you are the controlling agent of intuition will create more work and keep you from an expanded state of awareness. The primary point is that intuition happens through you, not as a result of your control. Your main task is to create a space for intuition to emerge. We will see that this is quite a task, in and of itself.

Intuition and the Collective Unconscious

Carl Jung*[1] had an idea that in each person's unconscious there is a part that is connected to humanity's unconscious as a whole. This he called the collective unconscious. For Jung

---

[1]All names that are starred are noted in the Who's Who section at the end of the book with a description of their contributions and references to their work.

there lived in the collective unconscious certain modes or ways of being that he called "archetypes." Each person, according to Jung, lives out a variety of these archetypes. For example, there is the archetype of the wildman: a fierce, primal strong man who lives in all humans.

If one does not become in touch with or "own" an archetype, then this archetype will basically operate out of control in one's unconscious. This can prompt certain emotional behaviors in people who are out of sync with their characters. For example, violent outbursts can happen if a person does not integrate this wildman. However, if a person admits that this fierceness is a part of his or her character, then this characteristic can be integrated and balanced by other archetypal traits in the person, such as sensitivity and compassion. Each person has a rich array of diverse characteristics, which are unifying in their whole.

An extension of Jung's collective unconscious notion is that there is hidden deep within each person a dimension that is interconnected to everything else, the deep self. This dimension is not localized in time and space. Hence, the acausal nature of intuition is explained. We can access this dimension by learning to use our intuition.

David Bohm: A Physicist's View of Reality

David Bohm* is a noted physicist aligned with the teachings of Krishnamurti,* a Hindu philosopher who established a spiritual teaching center in Ojai, California. Bohm has created a concept he calls "the enfolded and unfolded reality." With this as vocabulary he discriminates between concrete reality and expanded reality.

Bohm uses a chemical experiment to explain his meaning. In the experiment, a drop of dye is dropped into a liquid. You can see the drop of dye when you first put it in the liquid. When you stir the liquid one way, it becomes diffuse and there is no dye apparent in the liquid. If you stir the liquid back the opposite way, the dye *reappears* in the liquid.

Bohm tells us that when the dye is localized in the liquid then this is the unfolded reality. This is the concrete reality we deal in every day. For example, we all think that the table that we eat off of is solid. However, on an atomic level there are great spaces in the solid; millions of subatomic particles are passing through it at all times.

The enfolded reality is the state when the dye is distributed throughout the liquid. Our conscious mind cannot actually perceive this reality, but we have a sense of it. This enfolded reality exists simultaneously with our "concrete" reality, but it can only be accessed through developing our intuitive force.

The Hindu Reality

Related to Jung, and Bohm, is the Hindu view of the mind (see figure 3). Hindu thought is quite clear on the need to make the unconscious mind conscious through refining the intuition. It is also instructive on what we might call the healthy ego and the controlling ego.

There are several divisions of the mind in Hindu thought. These include the sensory motor mind (the *manas*), the memory bank (the *chittas*), and a sense of stability in the self (the *ahankar*). In psychological terms, the ahankar could be termed "the healthy ego." The ahankar is essential to our development. By developing this healthy ego we gain a strong sense of ourselves, where we begin and end. Its development

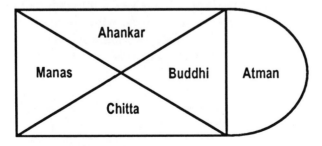

Figure 3. Hindu view of the mind.

makes us think that we are somebody. It also helps us integrate sensory perception from a stable viewpoint. It gives us confidence in moving into the material world. Ken Wilbur* notes that some individuals never develop a stable sense of self and this translates into mental illness. These people never know where they end and other people begin. To create psychological health, the ego or ahankar has an important place in building emotional strength. The part of the mind that stabilizes a person might be termed the healthy ego.

Another Hindu mind division is the *buddhi* or wisdom. This part of the mind is developed by learning to focus the mind's energy in the body. For example, in yoga the attention is focused on the body as it assumes rigorous physical positions. Similarly, the chitta (memory bank) is allowed to unwind as the attention stays with the body. This serves to make the unconscious conscious, as mind energy used to keep things hidden is released through this process.

Hindu spiritual practice—yoga,[2] for example—is designed to make the unconscious mind conscious. This is done by focusing the mind's attention on the body in yoga postures, or *asanas*. Focusing the attention in this way serves to trick the conscious mind into letting go of its hold on reality. During the asanas, the conscious mind has a task to do (i.e., pay attention to the body). Therefore, the conscious mind gives up judging what is real and unreal, since it is happily occupied. This creates an opening into the unconscious. The walls that separate the conscious from the unconscious are, in effect, relaxed. Unconscious material is released into conscious awareness and the process begins of destroying the barriers between the awareness in the conscious mind and the spirit self in the unconscious. Spiritual practice, as in yoga, medita-

---

[2]In Sanskrit, the word yoga means to yoke or bind. This is usually interpreted to mean yoking the mind, spirit and body. Yoga practice consists of eight levels or limbs. The third limb is asana, or physical postures. Some people practice asana for physical, not spiritual development. However, in general, yoga's aim is to create spiritual growth.

tion, prayer, or drumming, also acts to merge the body's will with the attention, since the practitioner concentrates on something during the practice. This gives the practitioner well-developed attentional skills. These skills allow a person to keep focused during chaotic internal events, which may occur as the conscious mind's structures break apart.

By learning to focus our attention through spiritual practice, the *buddhi* (wisdom), or part of the mind connected to the spirit self, grows and connects us with the spirit or real self in the unconscious, the *atman*. This is the unique part of the person that lives in the unconscious and that is interconnected to all other life. This is the part of the mind that is contacted through our intuition.

When Eastern spiritual practices tell us to "get out of our head," the point is to relax the conscious mind's hold on reality. We need the conscious mind for building stability. However, problems occur when the conscious mind starts screening reality and making perceptions and emotions fit preconceived assumptions about how the world works. This is the controlling ego at work. Instead of stabilizing the individual, the ego skews the perception of reality to conform to its needs. In other words, at a certain point the need for stability grows out of control. Learning to use the intuition will counterbalance the effect of the controlling ego. Since intuition stems from the unconscious mind, it is a direct link to forces outside the controlling ego's domain. Therefore by developing the intuition, a person can foil the controlling ego, causing it to give up its struggle to create reality in its own image.

Maslow's Self-Actualizing Tendency

Abraham Maslow* was a psychologist influenced by Eastern thought and one of the founders of humanistic psychology. He created a pyramid of needs that he felt motivated people in their lives (see figure 4 on page 26). The needs that all

Figure 4. Maslow's need pyramid.

humans are motivated by are survival, safety, social acceptance, self-esteem, and self-actualization. The needs progress
from survival on up. As each need was met, a person could
move up the pyramid to deal with the next set of needs. For
example, if people lived in a war zone or a famine region,
then they would not be dealing with esteem needs, they
would be consumed with survival. Even though people, in
general, work up through these levels of needs, a person can
move up and down across the levels and may be working at
all levels at the same time. A yogi in a cave may consciously
deny his or her survival needs to work at the actualization
level. A spiral may be a more apt graphic for the concept. In
a spiral a person works through each need and then returns
to them again and again at a more refined level.

Maslow's needs give strong support to the idea that it is
important to attend to the sense of self, or the healthy ego, in
order to build self-esteem. People need a stable sense of self
and love for the self before they can move to other needs. At
the top of Maslow's needs pyramid is self-actualization. At
this point a person comes in contact with the spiritual self

and transcends the individual ego. It's as if the individual ego needs to be nurtured, embraced, and loved, and then released to the universe. Maslow's need hierarchy may be like the Zen monk's hundred-step ladder. With patience the monk slowly climbs to the top. Then, the task is to jump. If a person does not eventually take this step of transcendence, then he or she holds on to separation and can never fully be whole with the deep spirit inside. The force that drives the individual through the needs is termed the actualizing tendency. This is an unconscious force and could be seen as similar to the atman or Jung's deep self.

An analogous view to Maslow's is the Hindu circle view of the self (see figure 5). In this model, the person consists of a series of circles which are concentric. The outer circles deal with the grosser levels of existence, very similar to Maslow's safety and physical needs. A person can move through the circles by developing a focus in the mind through meditation or yoga practice. This acts to quiet the conscious mind and lets the intuition emerge. In the center one contacts a more subtle or non-material energy level. This most inward circle is the atman.

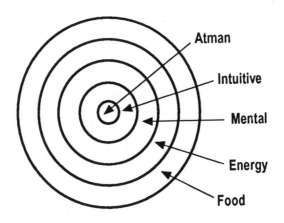

Figure 5. The Hindu circle view of the self.

The Mind and Intuition

The models we have discussed explain how the mind works and how it interfaces with reality. They include Jung's collective unconscious, Bohm's enfolded-unfolded reality, Maslow's pyramid of needs, and the Hindu mind divisions and circles. The following list reminds us of the important points to remember across these models.

- The conscious mind has a strong purpose in creating a stable sense of self and communicating reality to others.

- A healthy ego is necessary to one's emotional development.

- At a certain point the ego gets out of control and wants to control it all.

- The conscious mind will try to make perceptions and emotions *fit* what it has created as reality.

- The perceptions of the conscious mind are not necessarily reality.

- There is a deep[3] self hidden in the unconscious, which when contacted through intuition can reveal expanded realities.

- This deep self is interconnected to all other life and occupies a dimension beyond time and space.

- The intuition is the way to contact the deep self.

---

[3]Note that deep self and spirit self are used interchangeably in this manuscript. Deep self is from the Jungian tradition and spirit self is from the Hin-du tradition. Higher self is not used to reinforce the concept that the spiritual path is moving into one's humanity as opposed to overcoming it.

How to Work with Your Intuition

The best way to activate the intuition is to adopt a spiritual practice, since these practices teach a focus of attention. Spiritual practices include yoga, meditation, prayer or any repetitive, rhythmic activity that does not seek meaning and that is used with the intention of increasing spiritual awareness. The purpose of spiritual practice is to quiet the conscious mind and create a space within the mind. With much practice, this unconscious mind can be kept open. When this occurs expanded awareness results and the intuition is active in providing insights from the spirit self to the unconscious.

Getting the conscious mind to let go of its hold on reality is tricky. The conscious mind is a master at figuring out how to fit things into the boxes it has made. There are structures in the mind that support our notion of who we are. People like Sigmund Freud* have taught us that our mind is like an hydraulic system. We have a given amount of energy in our mind and when certain things happen that are traumatic or do not fit with our assumptions then the energy in the conscious mind is used to move these experiences into the unconscious. This depletes the amount of energy available for our development. Over time, if more and more issues and experiences are pushed into the unconscious, the mind does not have enough energy to take care of daily functioning, let alone spiritual development. The mind becomes pressurized as in an hydraulic system. Defense mechanisms act to maintain this pressurized state. These mechanisms suppress experiences that challenge the mind's view of reality. To release energy that is tying up the unconscious, practices are necessary to give space for the intuition to operate. Some principles of working with the intuition and disarming these mechanisms can be derived from spiritual practice:

1) *Allow the process.* Instead of trying to contact the unconscious, use a passive process of quieting the mind by focus-

ing the attention. This is not easy; it is quite difficult "to allow."

2) *Suspend judgment.* This is critical. As long as you are trying to figure out what is good or bad, what is real or unreal and what something means, then you are giving energy to your conscious mind to maintain its hold on reality. You must develop what the Buddhists term "detachment," or learning to watch what happens in the mind without reaction. It is alive detachment—you are allowing yourself to feel whatever comes up. You are not denying feelings. But you do not judge your feelings or thoughts.

3) *Trust the deep self.* The actualizing tendency in the unconscious will lead you to positive growth. We contact this deep self with our intuition not with our conscious mind.

4) *Trust your body reaction.* Your physical body holds the ancient wisdom of the Earth. The body is made out of the material that was in the Earth when it began and is the product of centuries of evolution. It contains the mysteries that made the Earth. Your body never lies. Psychologists tell us that eighty percent of what we communicate comes from the nonverbal cues of the body and face, not from our words. Hatha yoga (the form of yoga that includes arduous physical positions or asanas) teaches us that the body is a microcosm of the universe. As we learn to bring our awareness to the body then we learn to bring our awareness to the universe. *Hatha* actually means sun and moon, and *yoga* means to yoke or to bind. Therefore *Hatha yoga* means to yoke two opposing forces, which could be interpreted as bringing the mind into the body.

Bodywork therapies (i.e., Reiki, Rolfing) rest on the assumption that emotional traumas are stored in the body. By relaxing and releasing sites of the trauma in the body, we can then release these emotions. Therefore bringing your attention to the body and sensing its reactions is fundamental to working with your intuition. Intuition, in fact, may be the same as the body sense. By bringing the attention to the body, a person improves and gains skills in using the intuition.

Imagery Exercise: Body Relaxation

Begin by feeling your body slowing down and becoming warmer. Take your attention to the very tips of your toes. See a multi-colored butterfly land on the tip of your right big toe. When it lands, it turns on a little cell at the very end of the toe. You feel a slight charge at the end of this toe. The butterfly now lands on the second toe on the right foot, then the middle toe, the fourth toe, and the little toe. Each time the butterfly lands you feel a cell turn on at the end of the toe. Your energy moves out through the feet and the toes of your right foot.

The butterfly moves to your left big toe. A cell turns on. Then the butterfly moves to your second toe, your middle toe, your fourth toe, and your fifth toe. The toes on your left foot feel alive. You feel energy pouring down your left leg and into your left foot.

The butterfly flies up to your right thumb, a cell turns on. It proceeds to your right index, middle, ring, and little finger. You feel the palm of your right hand energized. This palm feels heavy and warm. The butterfly moves over to your left thumb. Then it moves to your left index, middle, ring, and little finger. You feel the cells on the tip of your left hand become alive. The palm of your left hand feels heavy and warm.

Take your attention to your right shoulder joint. Go deep inside this joint with your attention. Imagine that you are making space between the bones inside this joint. See a yellow color in the joint. Then see that color move across your chest and down into your left hip joint. Take your attention deep into the hip joint. See the bones; imagine that you create a space in this joint.

At this point move your attention to your left shoulder joint. Visualize the forms of the bones in this joint, and move your attention deep inside this joint. Open this joint. See a blue or greenish blue color in this joint. Then move this color across your chest and down into the right hip joint. See this blue or greenish color move into the right hip joint around the bones. Open this joint.

Feel the energy move from the right hip joint into the right thigh, into your kneecap, and down your right calf. Feel this energy pour out your right foot. Feel a continuous energy from your left shoulder joint across your chest through your right hip joint and down your leg and into your right foot. Imagine a similar feeling beginning in your right shoulder joint. Move this energy across your chest and into your left hip joint. Then imagine this energy pouring into your left leg, your kneecap, down your calf, and emptying into your left foot. The energy continues and pours out your left foot.

Take your attention to the base of your spine. *Very slowly* have your attention move up your spine, vertebra by vertebra. Imagine that the vertebrae move apart and a space grows between each bone in your spinal column. Think about the curve in your lower back and the curve at your neck. Realize that these curves are good and help you as a human stand upright. Move your attention to these curves. Thank and caress them.

Release the tension in your neck. Imagine that you are standing up to your neck in a body of warm, gently swaying water. Feel the tension in your neck release as you feel the water swaying around your neck. See a bud of a lily floating in the water in the middle of your neck. As you focus on it, the lily blooms.

Relax the back of your head, the top of your head. Think about your eyeballs. Feel them sink into your head. Feel the round muscles around your eyes relax. Feel your nose flatten as it moves into your face. Relax your cheeks and your lips. Unlock your jaw. Relax your tongue and throat. Feel a spot under your right ear open. Feel a spot under your left ear open. Feel your whole body getting heavier, warmer, softer.

Feel a sense of your body and notice how wonderful your energy is. Give thanks to your body for the journey it has and will take you on. Now take your attention throughout your body to notice how it feels. Stay with a deep feeling of calm for awhile. Then slowly come back to your day-to-day reality. Carry the peace you've felt inside with you throughout your day.

Imagery Exercise: Transforming Pain

This imagery exercise is not a panacea. It will not remove the physical cause of pain, but it will release emotional issues associated with a particular pain.

Sit or lie comfortably. Take your attention inside your body. Think of a place in your body where you often feel pain. Slowly and carefully take your attention to that part of your body.

Where is it? Is it inside or on the skin surface? Is it in a muscle, or a bone, or in an organ? How big a space does this pain take up? Take your attention as carefully as you can to this space and sense the spot where the pain is.

Now what would the pain look like? Keep your attention at the space of the pain. Create a symbol or metaphor for the pain. It can actually be physiological, or it can be a symbol that stands for the pain. If you do not see anything, this is fine. You possibly have a sense of the pain. Also, if you take your attention there, you may see a vague form, or a color. Keep looking at the form or color and more details will come to you.

Give yourself permission to transform, change, or shift the symbol. Let your attention tap the healing force in your unconscious. Let the symbol of the pain change.

Stay with it. Give it time. Let your deep self have its way. Trust the process.

Now take your attention back to the spot of the pain. Very, very slowly sense this spot again. How does it feel now? If there is no change that is fine. But return to this spot across the next several days. Watch the spot and see if the symbol changes. Now bring your attention back to this time and space. Carry the depth of your inner being with you.

Imagery Story:
Mark and the Decaying Mass in the Stomach

Mark felt some pain in his stomach. It was very tight. It was as if it had been hit repeatedly, and it had become very hard and crusty as a result.

When Mark took his attention inside his stomach, he found that it looked like a very large hole. It was an enormous space. At the bottom of the space was a black crust, almost like the black of volcanic tar pits.

Mark gave himself permission to change the image. He wanted to remove the tar. He took off a layer and then another layer as if he was scraping it. Finally there were cracks in the black, and he could see red in the cracks, oozing up. He let the space bleed. This would clean the wound. He was then able to combine all the remaining black into a ball. He wanted to take the ball out of his stomach. As soon as he took the ball out of his stomach, it grew immediately into a gigantic mountain in front of him. Mark felt a release in his stomach. It felt raw, but it was not decaying.

It doesn't matter what Mark thought happened. It doesn't matter what these symbols mean in the conscious mind. The deep self presented the metaphors of the problem and also presented symbols for changes and transformation. By letting go of figuring out the meaning of these symbols, it is possible to keep this process in the unconscious without dealing with the constraints of the conscious mind. In this case, there were many emotional wounds stored in the stomach region. These were old and so suppressed that a crust was needed to keep them repressed. When released these wounds grew into a mountain.

Chapter Three

Imagery

I was lying on the ground in the forest. I felt a part of the Earth that I held in my hands. As I moved my hands and toes into the dirt, the texture and smell was very vivid. It was as if my visual field was filled with crystals and grains of dirt. I was lying naked on the ground and feeling alone and helpless. But I liked the dirt and how it felt. It was warm and held me as a mother holds her child. A gigantic bird appeared. It was all white and had legs like a man. The feathers were very luminous, like the crystals in the dirt. It came toward me, but I was not afraid. The bird picked me up in his mouth and began flying. Soon I was in a nest high on the mountain. I noticed the sticks of the nest very clearly. These sticks were as big around as my forearm. I noticed that I was lying in the nest with the Eagle's other children. I liked being there. It felt safe and secure. I knew that some day I would need to be strong and go out on my own. But not for awhile. I was safe now.

The Balanced Being

There are many descriptors for the role of imagery in the human psyche (mind and soul):

- the voice of the unconscious;
- the primitive language of the brain;
- the medium for multiple realities;
- the conduit of visions from the spirit world;

As a thought form, imagery plays a function in each of the four aspects of the human being—the mind, body, emotions, and spirit. Thinking in images or internal sensations of sight, sound, movement, touch, smell, or taste opens the mind beyond the strictures of conscious thought, which must create a concrete reality and decide what is right and wrong.

If space can be created in the mind, and judgment can be suspended, then the four aspects of the being can become balanced and take their rightful place in the interplay of consciousness (see figure 6). Imagery, by focusing the attention, serves to create this space.

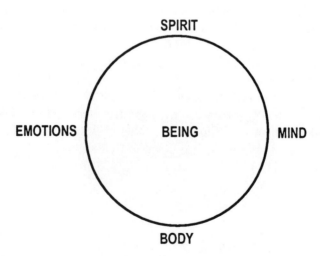

Figure 6. The four aspects of the being in balance.

In figure 6, the conscious mind has relinquished its control, so that each aspect of the being is balanced in a person's awareness. Awareness here is the space in the mind that is created when the attention is focused as in a spiritual practice or in imaging. Practicing imagery can have the same effect as a spiritual practice, since the attention is focused on a sensation in the mind. Most people think of their awareness as the thoughts in their conscious mind; this is not the case. Awareness is the attention that creates an openness to the moment of experience.

The term conscious mind was used in the last chapter to explain the part of the mind that contains thoughts. This is distinguished from consciousness, which is a person's entire inner experience. This inner experience includes the thoughts of the conscious mind as well as all other inner experiences, the sensations of the body, emotions, or visions of the spirit.

Very few people have their awareness balanced across the four being aspects since certain aspects are buried deep within the unconscious. Therefore, people are asleep to cer-

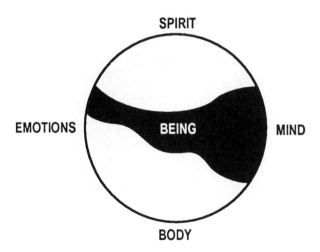

Figure 7. A typical Westerner's consciousness. The dark section signifies awareness.

tain aspects of their being. For example, the typical Westerner's consciousness is primarily in the mind and is only in a part of the emotions, as demonstrated in figure 7, on page 39.

Some other people in the West are very aware of their spiritual aspect and also the thoughts in their mind. These people are often attracted to spiritual practices—either traditional ones or those of the new age. The drawing of their four aspects might look like figure 8.

There are many other combinations as well. It might be interesting to draw where the aspects of your being lie in your conscious experience. Are you aware of the thoughts in your mind? Or the sensations in your body? Your emotions? Or your unity with all life?

Each aspect has its role in the human persona. Each must have play and balance with the others to create a whole human living in harmony with nature and spirit. This creates wholeness of the being, as in the original drawing.

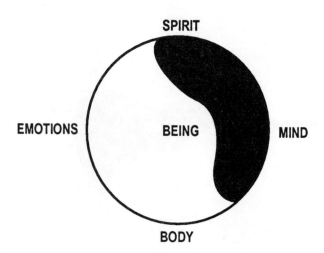

Figure 8. A consciouness aware of the spiritual and the mental aspects.

The practice of imagery can be the process and path to this harmony.

1) Imagery can move the mind into the body. This gives a solid basis for intuitive work, since the body holds the mysteries of creation.

2) Imagery can move the mind into the emotions using the body as a point of departure. Sensing emotions in the body is the most reliable way to stay out of the mind's conscious hold on reality. Emotions are also the bridge to clarity of intuition, since as "sensations," emotions are similar in topography to intuition. Therefore they are often confused with intuition. Learning to sense emotions vividly will sharpen intuitive skills, and eventually help an individual distinguish between an emotional and an intuitive sensation.

Imagery and Science

Imagery might be called a culturally appropriate Western spiritual practice because science can verify its effects. It is documented in Western scientific research that through imagery people can:

- increase levels of given cells and endorphin levels;

- lower blood pressure;

- sharpen sports performance;

- produce creative discoveries in science and the arts;

- enhance the memory;

- heal emotional trauma;

- create visions that give a sense of well-being and bliss.

Imagery creates an inclusive space where the aspects of the being can come together and balance. Imagery then acts to balance the being by bringing information from the unconscious to the conscious. Imagery could be a Western-friendly practice that contacts the spirit self in the unconscious. No Eastern guru or even a crystal are required. Through imagery the person taps the deep self which naturally develops the spirit.

The following sections provide detail on the role of imagery in human cognition in the four aspects of the being - the mind, body, emotions, and spirit.

Imagery and the Mind

Thinking in images is a natural human cognitive process. This means that all humans image or can produce an internal perceptual sensation in the mind, such as a noise, a vision, a smell, a movement, a taste, or a touch.

Just for a moment think of the face of someone you love. Notice the contour of the individual's cheek. Reach out and touch this person's cheek. Hear the person say your name. In the image that just occurred in your mind you have had a visual, tactile, and auditory image.

Now think of coming home after an outing. Notice your front door. Feel your hand moving out and grasping the door knob. Notice how smooth the doorknob feels in your hand. As you walk into the house, you notice a smell that is your favorite dish cooking. You walk into the kitchen and realize that the dish is ready to eat. You get a fork and taste this favorite food. In this image, you used the senses of movement (kinesthesia), touch (tactile), smell (olfactory), and taste (gustatory).

In the above images, you may have noticed that the vividness of the senses varied. You may not have perceived some images at all. Everyone has his or her own way of imaging. That is why the word imagery is used instead of visualization, since the process is multisensory and does not only rely on the sense of vision. However, some people use visualization to denote an imagery process that is aimed at creating an event (i.e., increase cell levels).

A story from a physician who runs a stress reduction clinic at Stanford explicates that the imagery process is different for different people. This man, who we will call Dr. Stress, ran a clinic that helped hyertensive executives learn to relax in order to combat the probability of heart attacks. He taught the patients to image, since when a person thinks in images the heart rate and blood pressure automatically decrease. Imagery was a central part of the curriculum. However, Dr. Stress began to feel a little hypocritical because he had never actually seen an image in his mind. He experimented with a sensory deprivation tank and after twelve hours, he saw his first visual image—an upside down Exxon sign. This was a bit of a disappointment. After a time, though, it occurred to him he had done it in the past. He realized he had learned to fly a plane with kinesthetic images. He had rehearsed the movements of flying the plane in his mind. Dr. Stress' imagery experience was unique since he only imaged with the kinesthetic sense. Each individual's imagery style will also be unique.

Creativity

Creativity is not a process of the conscious mind; the mysteries of recombination, synthesis, and new expression reside in the unconscious. Psychologists document the stages of creativity as including: 1) data collection, 2) a period of waiting or incubation, 3) insight, and 4) verification. An example of this is the scientist who discovered that muscles move through an electrical process. He had collected data for years and had a hunch that electrical currents passed through muscles to make them move. After several years of inquiry, he had a dream about an experiment to test this theory. He woke up in the night and scribbled down notes. However in the morning he could not read the notes. This happened several nights, and finally on the third night, he could read his note. The notes described an experiment in which frog legs were put in a solution and an electrical voltage was then passed through the solution. He tried the method and it worked—the legs moved. His stages were:

1) Data Collection—he read and experimented.

2) Incubation—he waited several years.

3) Insight—he had a dream or an image from his unconscious on how to prove his hunch.

4) Verification—he conducted the experiment.

Imagery is central to creativity because it is how the unconscious speaks to the conscious mind. The underlying matrix of the unconscious mind (the creative force of the deep self) works on the problem, and then presents a solution in the form of an image. Einstein supposedly discovered relativity when he was riding on a streetcar in Bern, Switzerland. As he was riding, he had a vision of what it would be like to travel at the speed of light and realized that no time would pass.

The physiological basis for producing creative insight resides in the limbic system. Remember that the limbic system of the brain mediates memory, bringing information in and out of the unconscious. This system is also involved in intuition, or providing a holistic sense of what is happening. Imagery can then activate limbic function in pulling out pertinent memories and putting them together in a holistic manner.

Memory

An instructional methodology designed to accelerate memory uses imagery. "Superlearning" or "Suggestology," developed by G. Lozanov,[1] a Bulgarian physician, can speed the acquisition of a foreign language remarkably by creating retention of the language over a long period of time. Lozanov used techniques that created a state of relaxation and receptivity. These procedures included having people see images of themselves as successful learners and at the same time listening to Baroque largo music, which has the same beats per minute (60) as the human heartbeat at rest. A music therapist at Southern Methodist University, Michael Rider,[2] reports that the human body's rhythms (i.e., heart rate), "entrains" or matches the rhythm external to the body. This means that if the human body senses a rhythm of sixty beats per minute, it will try to match its heartbeat to this rhythm. The limbic system, which mediates imagery, is also rhythmic in nature since autonomic nervous system functions are regulated by the hypothalamus, the master gland of the body. This gland is located next to the limbic system in the physiology of the brain, and as such is affected by its function. Imagery and rhythm in Suggestology learning methods are combined to assist the memorization of material in an accelerated fashion.

Imagery techniques have been used since the time of Greek orators to memorize things. To experience this, try playing the game "I'm going to New York and I'm taking a toothbrush." Each person adds something to take to New York, but before that is added, the items that others have suggested must be repeated in the order that they were suggested. Play the game twice. The first time you play it, play it without trying any specific imagery technique. The next time you play it try to visualize or image in another modality (i.e., touching each object). Note the difference in the two approaches.

---

[1] Lozanov, G. *Suggestology and Outlines of Suggestopedy*. (New York: Gordon and Breach, 1978).
[2] Rider, M.S., Floyd, J.W., and Kirkpatrick, J. 1985. "The Effect of Music, Imagery and Relaxation on Adrenal Corticosteroids and the Re-entrainment of Circadian Rhythms." *Journal of Music Therapy*. 12: 46-58.

Sports Performance

Possibly the first documented effect of imagery was a study in 1949 by W. Twining[3] in the *Research Quarterly*. This study showed that practicing dart throwing with mental rehearsal improved performance just as well as practicing dart throwing by actually throwing a dart. Imagery has become a central practice in sports psychology. Most athletes travel with their sports psychologists, who have them image the actual motions required to sharpen performance. This is called kinesthetic imagery.

A structure in the limbic system, called the hippocampus, deals with spatial motor memories. By using imagery, a person can directly talk to the part of the mind that remembers movements. This also sharpens motivation and the arousal of the mind and body, since attention is also mediated by the limbic area. Imagery strengthens the mind-body connection, honing the athletes' abilities.

Healing Trauma

Researchers such as Charles Jordan[4] in a 1984 issue of the *Journal of Mental Imagery* have documented the effectiveness of imagery therapy. Jordan says that the amygdala, a rim-like structure under the cortex, transfers perceptions from body responses to the cortex, and that the actual neural connections are sparse. This explains the difficulty, at times, of sensing and integrating emotional experience. Since imagery also activates the limbic system, it can vivify an emotional experience to bring it fully into the conscious mind. Imagery can also open memories in the unconscious by activating the amygdala, the conduit of emotional memories. By bringing

---

[3] Twining, W. E. 1949. "Mental Practice and Physical Practice in Learning a Motor Skill." *Research Quarterly* 20: 432-435.
[4] Jordan, C.S. 1984. "Psychophysiology of Structural Imagery in Post-Traumatic Stress Disorders." *Journal of Mental Imagery* 8: 51-66.

the emotions to the conscious mind, imagery allows a force in the unconscious to heal and integrate the emotions.

The Ecstatic Experience

In his 1987 book, *The Psychology of Meditation*, Michael West[5] locates the source of ecstasy in the right hippocampus, the part of the brain mediating imagery. Imagery appears to be the medium of ecstasy and the medium of shamans. Shamans are spirit healers who journey to multiple realities and bring back symbols of healing. Rhythm is often the fuel that drives these journeys. All of this makes sense physiologically. Rhythm activates the limbic system in its interaction with autonomic nervous system functioning. Rhythm also seems to quiet the conscious mind in the cortex and speaks to the limbic system. Through imagery, mediated by the limbic system, a person can chart multiple realities and the dimensions of the collective unconscious.

Imagery may also activate the hot spots for endorphin creation in the limbic system. This may be the physiology that accompanies peak altered states of consciousness, which include bliss, harmony, and peace.

Imagery and rhythm not only enhance memory, promote relaxation, awaken creativity, and activate immune response, but also create altered and expanded consciousness of states of union and bliss. Imagery is truly the language of the mind, body, emotions, and spirit, and it creates a space in the mind for each of the four aspects to find its balance.

Imagery Work Assumptions

Assumption 1: There is an underlying force outside of our conscious mind. This force has been called the atman, the actual-

---

[5] West, M. *The Psychology of Meditation* (Atlanta, GA: Clarendon Press, 1987).

izing tendency, the Holy Spirit within, the creative force, the deep self, and the higher self. This force cannot be contacted with the conscious mind or the controlling ego because the controlling ego's function is to build an individual identity apart from the shared spirit within each person. Therefore there is an implicit resistance of the conscious mind to surrender its control and to open its awareness to this force, which connects every person to each other.

The existence of this force is important, because it means that the conscious mind does not need to "drive" or be in control of the imagery process. Many people who use visualizations to get what they want are using the conscious mind to control and create a world that fits their ego needs. The point here, and this cannot be overemphasized, is that the control of the conscious mind will interfere with the underlying healing force in the unconscious. Therefore a person using imagery work for spiritual development must surrender conscious control to build awareness of the deep self.

Assumption 2: This force can be contacted through imagery. Imagery can actually be seen as the voice of the deep self, or the screen within the mind on which the deep self shines its insights. Jeanne Achterberg calls imagery the primitive voice of the mind. Since it is a primitive language it can move in and out of the unconscious at will, exposing memories and facts to be recombined in creative insights and opening up suppressed trauma still to be healed from early childhood experiences. Imagery as primitive mind language also talks directly to body functions controlled by the autonomic nervous system, such as heart and breath rate.

Assumption 3: The force has a life of its own that is positive and healing in nature. It can be trusted. A cognitive psychologist, Zenon Pylyshyn,[6] says that imagery accesses an underlying matrix in the mind, a matrix that operates outside of con-

---

[6] Pylyshyn, Z. 1981. "The Imagery Debate: Analogue Media Versus Tacit Knowledge." *Psychological Review* 88: 16-45.

scious control. This is a very interesting statement for a Western scientist whose scientific paradigm would reject the notion of a spiritual force active in cognition.

Pylyshyn was only interested in images in the mind and their relation to visual perception. He studied visual perception by examining the difference between actual vision and internal images in the mind. He found that people would shift the visual image in the mind, rotate it, and transform it without conscious direction. There also seemed to be a tendency of the mind to focus on a small detail of an image to bring it into focus. A force in the mind was propelling this imagery process.

Adopting the assumption that there is an underlying force in imagery work can be very useful. It allows a person to surrender conscious control of the image by believing that there is still some part of the mind, possibly the spirit, which is operative and will guide the imagery process. This force in the unconscious mind will present images of problems that need to be worked on, and then integrate information that is presented.

Painful events that have been buried in the unconscious can be opened only when the person is ready. When these memories are opened and re-experienced in an image, then the deep self begins the healing process, just as naturally as the body heals a cut on the hand. Sometimes the wounds are so large that a person needs help in feeling safe enough to open the wound. At this point seeking a therapist's help is in order. A good therapist will not fix or heal the wound with his or her own energy, but will help a person catalyze the inner healing force.

There are several ways the deep self may operate to heal a wound. These could include:

1) balancing the pain with a strength elsewhere in the persona;

2) assisting a person in feeling the pain completely, so that the issues associated with the pain are dispersed.

3) exposing a pattern of helplessness or victimization that, when experienced, prompts an individual to realize that the pattern is no longer necessary.

4) radiating the pain with love.

5) providing symbols of strength or acting to transform images of the pain into images of healing.

6) creating a bird's-eye viewpoint of the experience in order to prompt understanding through detachment.

Imagery can also reveal karmic patterns that are motivating a person's life. A karmic pattern is a basic assumption of who the person is. One pattern could be "I am unworthy," and another could be "Other peoples' needs are more important than mine." The karma could be based on past lives, karma inherited from parents, or karma created in this life. These patterns are usually driven by some archetype such as a martyr, warrior, victim, or villain. When these patterns are released from the unconscious into conscious awareness, then the deep self may discard the pattern as being no longer necessary. This may need to happen at deeper and deeper levels many times before the pattern is actually released.

It is helpful to open to the imagery experience, bond with the images by feeling the emotions evoked, and wait for images to move of their own accord. After the imagery experience you continue to suspend judgment of the experience and to then wait for insight.

Not seeking the meaning of an image also allows a person to experience images that may seem dark or frightening without retreating from the image. The person knows a force inside of him or her is guiding the process and is healing in nature. This allows early traumas to be presented and released or integrated. It also sets the stage for karmic patterns to be revealed and released, so that they cease to drive the person's behavior.

Assumption 4: The kinesthetic or body reaction is the most reliable check on what is happening in imagery work. The body reaction to an image is the place to start in determining what is happening within the image. The body is the most reliable source of intuition. When you get a body sense about something you can trust it. Therefore, to prevent yourself from "getting too much into your head" about an image, you can move your attention into your body during or after an image to get a reliable message from the image.

In addition, actually attending to your body sense will teach you to image better. As you learn to move your attention into your body you develop the focus of attention that is needed to image in a vivid manner. Focusing the attention with repeated practice also creates a space in the mind that allows the images freer mobility out of the unconscious.

How to Lead Imagery

Many professionals, after experiencing the profound effects of imagery, may want to use imagery with the people they work with. The following guidelines are aimed at helping people learn to lead imagery with others. The guidelines can also be used by a person to improve his or her own imagery process. Imagery can be used for many things, but regardless of the specific purpose, there are points that will vivify the imagery experience. The following are basic goals of leading imagery.

1) Get the person to bond with the image or to become totally immersed. If this happens, the mind interprets this as a "real" experience. It is done by encouraging *perceptual* features of the image, like "What color is the shirt you are wearing?" "Notice how your foot feels as you move." Kinesthetic and tactile senses are critical to this process.

2) Help the person create a vivid image. This is done by freeing the person of any expectations of what the image should be like. Assure people that whatever happens is okay, even if they do not image. Also they can sit however they like, as long as they do not have to move during the imagery. Eyes can be open or closed. Using relaxation instructions before imagery and using rhythm either through drumming or music are highly effective in vivifying imagery.

3) Assist the person in allowing the images to move of their own accord. This is done by using a very slow delivery style and long pauses. If you track the image in your own mind as you are leading it, you can gauge how much time is needed. Also you will find that your intuition is enhanced as you lead imagery. You will often feel when it is time to add more information or to change a scene. It is important to key the first scene of the image in detail and lead people to use all senses in this scene. After that you need to keep scenes simple and encourage body reaction in the image, like "How does that feel?" People often make the mistake of adding too much detail and creating many complicated scenes. This is probably because they do not trust the intuition in leading imagery. During the imagery, leave pauses in which you preface them by saying, "Now let the image move of its own accord."

4) Vivify the experience through rhythm. Drum at the beginning or play music during imagery.

Throughout the imagery experience, if you feel the energy is going well, you can praise effort. People seem to like this. You will find as you lead more and more imagery that your intuition becomes very keen and you can feel changes in the person as you are leading the experience. Also, you may have a certain plan for the imagery, but as you are in the middle of the imagery you sense something different or you actually see an image to describe. Go with this.

At the end of an imagery experience, it may be wise to close up the doors of the unconscious. If some major issue was revealed, it can be returned to and brought out again when the person is ready to deal with it. A good closing technique is for people to move their attention to each of their chakras or seven energy centers (defined in chapter four) and slightly pat each one with their attention. Another closing image is to have the person image him or herself in a comfortable chair at home, curling up as he or she becomes sleepy and covering up with a favorite blanket.

People seem to really enjoy talking about their imagery after it happens. Capitalize on this by giving people time and space to express their personal journeys. During debriefing it is important not to support people in figuring out the meaning of the image. Instead, ask people about their body senses or feelings from imagery. Assure the person that insight will come in time. Drawing or writing about the image in a journal can bring the insight to light. Staying away from figuring out the meaning of an image can be very difficult for some people. They will actively resist sensing an image in the body.

It is essential that everything is made "okay" in an imagery exercise. This serves to allow the deep self to be active in the imagery process. There are no expectations, no right or wrong images, no need to figure out what they mean, and no need to even image. The idea is to develop a sense of an inner experience. Imagery is best when it prompts a person to engage with the bare experience of the inner self and to then allow emergence. The purpose of imagery is not for you as a leader to fix or impose your agenda, rather to allow a person to evoke vivid images. These images can move of their own accord and provide insight to the conscious mind from the deep self.

Imagery Exercise: The Child

This imagery exercise shows that anything can happen in the image. You can have many selves and move in many realities. Changes in the images then create changes in the unconscious structures that motivate behavior in a person. Many times a given image must be returned to over and over to clear unresolved issues.

You are outside at a place you've been before, near the home you grew up in as a child. It could be a park or a meadow or another outside setting. You are walking in this scene and you begin to notice perceptual details. How does the ground feel under your feet? Is it windy? Does the wind move against your cheek? Do you notice any noises? Look down and notice the texture and color of what you are wearing. What color is the sky? What color is the earth? Reach out and touch a leaf!

Now you find a place to sit down that is comfortable. A little ways away from you, you notice a child playing. There is something very specific or noticeable about this child. There is something striking about the child. You notice this right away.

For a while the child does not notice you, and you watch as the child sits, plays, or proceeds with the activity at hand.

You notice a feeling in your heart as you watch the child. Pretty soon you realize that it is you as a child. Your adult self is watching your child self.

Soon the child notices you. Either the child approaches you or you approach the child. After a time the two of you talk or interact in some way.

Pretty soon you ask the child what he or she needs. If possible you try to provide that. If you are not ready to do that, that is okay. Often the child self wants to come and sit in the adult self's heart.

Let the imagery move of its own accord.

Let the imagery complete itself. Slowly come back to this time and space. Imagine yourself in a chair in your home late at night. You're warm and very sleepy. You cover yourself with a blanket. You feel safe and warm.

Imagery Story: Monica's Birth

Monica had a lot of issues with her mother but she could never figure out what was the matter. Her mother seemed like a warm, good, kind person. The perfect mother. But Monica was always mad at her mother underneath. Monica enjoyed covertly rejecting her mother, like not eating a meal that her mother had cooked especially for her. During a group imagery experience, Monica was asked to find a sensation of pain in her body. She found it in her left shoulder blade. She was asked to see how much space the pain took up and to see what it would look like if the pain had a form. During this imagery, the leader asked Monica to think back to an earlier time when she had had that pain. This exercise was repeated several times, so that Monica went back further and further in her life to trace the roots of her pain. The last image she had was coming out of a warm, soft, dark place into a bright room. She looked at her mother and her mother was bleeding out of a big hole. Monica thought she had killed her mother.

It was Monica's birth and she felt that she had killed her mother at her birth. No matter how kind or loving her mother was, Monica felt that her mother resented her. By seeing symbols of these feelings in her image, Monica could validate herself. The dynamics in her relationship with her mother not only included Monica's anger, but also resentment from her mother. Seeing this, helped Monica release fears that her mother had rejected her and helped her not to judge herself so harshly for her feelings about her mother.

In an imagery experience, it does not matter if the images actually have happened. Monica's image of her birth was highly significant. It symbolized the dynamics in her unconscious which, when accurately sensed, helped to dispel misconceptions.

Chapter Four

Emotions

I was in Japan for a psychological conference. I had gone a few days early
to orient myself to the country. Everyone said people spoke English
in Japan. But in Fukuoka, they
didn't. It had been three days in
which I had not talked to other
people. My *chitta* (the Hindu term
for the memory bank in the unconscious mind) had been unwind-
ing. All my negative thoughts about
myself came out like a torrent, as I made a
fool of myself in this highly civilized culture.

I didn't expect to have a spiritual experience in Japan; I
was there to give a talk and advance myself professionally.
But since I had been doing yoga for 15 years, I had an interest in Eastern spiritual practice. I wanted to visit Buddhist
temples. I found one and entered.

The steps up to the main floor were tall and shiny. I took
off my shoes and walked towards the huge Buddha that was
painted on the wall. I knelt and centered myself. I asked the
Buddha to forgive me for all the negative thoughts I had about
myself. The Buddha immediately entered my heart and rended
it open. The physical sensation was like childbirth. And inside
my heart as he tore it open, the Buddha filled me with enormous waves of compassion which were ecstatic and orgiastic.
I lay prone in front of the Buddha, sobbing. The energy was

so deep and powerful I found it necessary to lie down. When I finally left, a monk came out and offered me kleenex. I thought that maybe I was to give a donation, so I offered him money. He waved it away. His act too was an act of compassion. I didn't need forgiveness for my negativity; I needed the compassion lying dormant in my own heart awakened.

Emotions and the Spiritual Path

Emotions are critical to learning to work in expanded consciousness, primarily because most people deny their emotions in order to conform to some idealized notion of spirituality. People think that when they become "spiritual" and learn to deal in other realities, they will become strong and powerful. Hidden in the idea of becoming strong and powerful is the value that being emotionless is good. People have a vision of an Eastern guru or even a Christ who sits in a very relaxed manner and dispenses teachings from a calm and serene face. This "spiritual" person moves slowly, the voice is rarely raised, the guru doesn't sleep, has indefatigable energy, probably eats pure-type things like apples or yogurt, or maybe even lives on sunshine. The guru definitely doesn't get angry, sad, hurt, frustrated, irritated, or depressed. I use the male pronoun, because "he" is a he, unless of course "he" is Mother Teresa.

Often new-age magazines will have articles about emotions and the spiritual path. The gist of these articles usually goes like this: "Look at how calm and serene spiritual people in the East are. If one dies to one's ego, then one will be calm and serene like these folks in the East." These articles also include rational arguments about how one cannot be swayed by one's emotions if one is to be spiritual. Neither the editors nor the authors seem to notice that using rational arguments to explain non-rational emotions is like comparing oranges to apples.

Westerners are familiar with the phrase of "dying to one's ego," but they are not quite sure about what this really means. This concept of dying to the ego is used as a guiding principle by new agers on how to deal with emotions.

Ego death is interpreted as not being emotional. If you have died to your ego, which in the Western new-age culture means that you don't care about what happens to you, then you will always be calm and serene. The Western new-age culture also believes that what happens to you in this physical reality is a result of what you think. Your thoughts manifest reality. Holding these two assumptions at the same time creates a circular dilemma. You are not supposed to care what happens to you, but at the same time you have created what is happening to you.

A scenario such as the following can occur. You have worked very hard on a project at your job. Your boss cuts it apart, seemingly not reacting to your work, but responding from jealousy. You feel hurt and angry. This is not good, because if you had died to your ego, what someone else thinks about you would not matter. At the same time you probably created this situation by some deep feelings of your own unworthiness. This is not good, either. If you would only love yourself more, then good things would happen to you.

As Ken Wilber* eloquently states, new-age thinking creates a modern version of Protestant guilt. Judging your feelings and assuming that you are responsible for situations that prompt negative feelings reinforces a sense of unworthiness and separation from God. There is a way out of this maze.

1) Learn what dying to the ego means, based on the teachings of ancient mystical traditions, both East and West. To do this you must learn to sense your emotions honestly and to let go of your expectations for what you want to happen.

2) Accept your human form completely, including all emotions that arise, using teachings from humanistic psychology as a guide. Humanistic psychology emerged in the mid-twen-

tieth century as a reaction to the view of a mechanistic, externally controlled human. It postulates that each person possesses an inherent force which when contacted will lead one to positive growth. Abraham Maslow and Carl Rogers are most closely associated with this movement.

Alive Detachment

Most people think that the Buddha's message that all suffering stems from attachments or expectations of what is to happen means that we are not supposed to feel. Lack of attachment is not the same as lack of feeling. To feel nothing a human being has to suppress feelings. Releasing attachments is not the same as denying feelings. People need to care about themselves in order to love others. Ancient spiritual traditions, particularly Christianity, are quite clear that loving oneself is central to the spiritual path. Following the Buddha's teachings of releasing expectations about outcomes is quite a different thing from not feeling.

In certain spiritual traditions, monastic ones for example, the assumption is that one must experience pain in order to release oneself from the human condition. Fasting, vows of poverty and celibacy are all examples of this. The Buddha tried these forms of deprivation in his search for enlightenment. However, it was not until he sat under the bodhi tree for many, many days that he became enlightened. My idea of what happened at that point was that he realized that instead of suffering to let go of outcomes, one can joyously surrender to the compassion of the universe. This is not the same as not caring what happens to you or not feeling.

Pain in the martyr sense can be used by the controlling ego as a badge of achievement. But no one is counting in the game of spiritual development. Every person has the same spiritual energy as every other human and possibly as every other tree or rock. Pain need not be pursued in and of itself as a way to be spiritual. Pain will come, since we probably would make no changes if we did not experience pain. Our system likes homeostasis. But pain is only another emotion. It is a friendly reminder to help us know where our attachments lie. Pain comes, and as we grow in our awareness we can use this pain as a messenger. When we feel pain it is a signal to let go of something. However, we don't need to pursue pain or take it as a judgment that we created a bad reality.

Alive attachment is embracing the human condition and feeling emotions fully. It is the practice of surrendering the desires that accompany the emotion. This is a paradox, and paradoxes continually present themselves in spiritual work. The paradox here is to feel and to let go of the outcome of the feelings, simultaneously. "I want this very much and it is okay if it does not happen." In this framework the person cares very much about what they want or feel, but lets go of the outcome of these feelings.

This is an important point, because many people want only to be serene on their path to realization. Many saints were dirty, wore rags, and giggled. Many Zen masters posed very silly questions to their students. You take the human experience as it comes moment by moment, realizing your spirituality by becoming fully human. Dying to the ego means to feel and to embrace the human condition, but to neutralize the controlling ego by letting go of what you want to happen.

Manifestations and Affirmations

It was noted above that the new-age movement teaches that what you experience is a result of what you think. This concept is then applied to what is called using affirmations to manifest (i.e., create) reality. For example, you affirm with a thought what you might want to happen, and supposedly this will then manifest for you. Affirmations usually take the form of statements. For example, "I rejoice in my existence," or "I am getting a new job" could both be affirmations. These can be esoteric or can be related to more material or practical things. Often events that one wants to happen are also visualized in the mind as one is saying the affirmation.

This practice of affirmations is most probably related to the ancient concept of karma. But it might be a Hollywood version of this concept. Karma essentially means that there is a reaction to an action. Sounds a little like a principle from physics, doesn't it? Supposedly an ancient Hindu holy book, the Rig Veda, contains information about the unity of energy, now being discovered by physicists. It is not a surprise, then, that a Hindu concept, such as karma, is a universal principle. As you might guess, such a universal principle will have many applications. For example, there can be the karma one creates in one's own lifetime, and there is karma that one has created across many incarnations. There is also inherited karma from one's parents, racial karma, national karma, and so forth.

But how does karma apply in the context of manifesting reality through affirmations? The new-age idea is that thinking is an action, therefore there will be a reaction to this thought in the world around you.

This is a bit simplistic for two reasons. The first reason is that many other people are thinking at the same time as you are thinking. Therefore the reactions to these thoughts can be varied and complex. What happens in the environment outside your mind may be the result of many individuals' karma, not just your own. You cannot blame yourself if bad things happen to you. It is not necessarily the result of your thoughts. On the other hand, on a cosmic scale the whole notion of bad and good doesn't exist. Therefore bad things don't really happen to you. It is just more grist for the mill, as Ram Dass* says.

The second reason that the new-age notion is simplistic is that the definition of thinking is not clear. Most people define thinking as the words that play in the conscious mind. However, a great deal of what happens in your mind is at an unconscious level. And for the most part, there is no way that you can even be aware of what you "think" in your unconscious mind. The atman or deep self is probably the part of the mind that manifests into reality. This means that our job is not to affirm in the conscious mind, but to contact the deep self by opening the conscious into the unconscious. We do this through spiritual practice not through affirmations.

The idea of affirmations can be okay, if an affirmation serves to align you with your deep self. This can be done with affirmations of self love, affirmations of surrendering to the universe, and so forth. But affirmations to achieve certain things on the physical plane may be counterproductive. You will probably get what you affirm, but it may create a sidestep on the path of uniting with your spirit self.

We do, however, manifest from the non-material or subtle realm to the material realm. There is no doubt about it. But we manifest from the deep self. And if we mean business about spiritual development, our task is to let go of the outcome of our wants and desires. Affirmations to manifest specific material things are avenues for our controlling ego to imprint on the physical plane. We must always be careful to neutralize the controlling ego, instead of empowering it.

Accepting the Self

Instead of working on affirmations to manifest things in one's life, one's job is to learn to be human. This is done by accepting all that is inside the human form. The paradox is that to be spiritual, one must be fully human. This means being emotional.

People often use spirituality to compensate for psychological issues of unworthiness and to mask suppressed trauma and pain with superiority. The need to be superior is almost always tied to deep feelings of unworthiness. It is a compensating mechanism of the controlling ego to create a sense of security, even though it will not be a true reflection of reality.

The physical, emotional, mental, and spiritual bodies of the person are all interrelated. Development in one body will have effects on the others. However, each element must have focus and attention for growth. Many people assume that if they put their attention into their spiritual development then all else will fall into place. The assumption is that if they become spiritual then they do not need to worry about emotional development. Jimmy Swaggert and even Rajneesh can teach us lessons about those types of assumptions. It is true that spiritual development will have an impact on the other bodies. The spiritual body will grow exponentially when given space within an individual's awareness. These surges of growth will exaggerate psychological issues that need to be released or healed, but you must still pay attention to these issues to heal the emotional body. This is of critical importance for people who want to work in expanded reality. The unconscious in effect needs to be "cleared" of emotional wounds that have been suppressed and of personality structures which skew perceptions to build false security. Humanistic psychology gives practical how-to's on ways to clear the mind of suppressed emotions.

Maslow's Needs

Abraham Maslow's* hierarchy of needs referred to in Chapter One has relevance to the issue of accepting the self and the emotions. Maslow's needs noted earlier were survival, safety, social acceptance, esteem, and self-actualization. Maslow believed that you could be in various need levels at the same time, but that an individual was propelled to meet each level. In other words, you could jump up and down on the need hierarchy, but you still had to meet each need. It would not work to attend only to self-actualization needs, which are primarily spiritual (i.e., states of unity and transcendence). You have to have a foundation to grow spiritually. This means that the esteem needs directly under self-actualization are critical to spiritual development. People have to be emotional before they can transcend. The emotional body needs room to grow; in most people the emotional body is atrophied since the controlling ego has shoved so much into the unconscious.

Fritz Perls,* another psychologist associated with humanistic psychology, also underscores the central aspect of emotional work. He pointed out a paradox that applies to working with emotions. You must accept an emotion before it will change. In order to heal emotional pain hidden in the unconscious, you must allow the emotions to emerge and sense them fully. Much of our work in being spiritual then is learning to be emotional. This can be transformed to spiritual work by learning to watch and feel without judgment. This is practicing alive detachment.

The way one meets Maslow's esteem needs is to accept whatever emotion that presents itself. This practice of accepting emotions is quite counter to both the U.S. and the new-age culture. Within both of these groups there are good and bad emotions. In the U.S. culture, strongly influenced by Protestant Christianity, good emotions are happiness and power or control. Anger is an okay emotion under certain conditions, particularly for men. In the new-age culture calmness and possibly pain are the two acceptable emotions. Other emotions are indicative of not being a good person. These may include vulnerability, weakness, sadness, rage, depression, and so forth. In order to be fully human, one must explode this value rating on emotions. Another paradox presents itself. The only way to change emotions is to feel them fully. This does not mean to act on the emotions, but rather to allow the sense of the emotion full play within the self. For example, if a person feels sadness, then he or she must stay with the sense of that feeling until it shifts or changes.

You can't be spiritual if you deny, suppress, or judge certain emotions. You have to jump into the experience of being human whatever comes up. You will have help in this process. Maslow's actualizing tendency, hidden in the unconscious, is a force that will help you heal and integrate emotions.

Healing Emotions

Carl Rogers,* the main proponent of counseling applications of humanistic psychology, teaches conditions to activate the actualizing tendency in order to work with emotions successfully. One of Roger's primary conditions for contacting a client's actualizing tendency was to totally accept the client. Another condition, which is an extension of acceptance, is to suspend judgment; whatever the client expresses is accepted without evaluation. This is congruent with what one learns to do in a spiritual practice such as yoga or meditation or prayer. You learn to keep the attention focused, watch, and not judge what is happening in the mind or body. This is how you develop the ability to create alive detachment.

With emotions, the practice of alive detachment is to feel or sense your emotions as fully as possible, but not to judge or react to this emotion. People want to say that they shouldn't have certain emotions. Or sometimes people will escape from an uncomfortable emotion by blaming the event or the person who evoked the emotion. Another avoidance tactic is to trip into another emotion. For example, a person who does not like feeling hurt may unconsciously move to anger without even feeling the hurt.

Emotions and Metaphors

Takeshi Masui,* a Japanese psychologist, has created a technique for working with emotions which accomplishes sensing the emotion without judging it. The technique relies on imagery. A person is led to create an image or symbol of an emotion in the part of the body where the emotion is felt. Then the person is asked to change the emotion symbolically without trying to figure out the meaning. The image of the emotion is changed. This keeps the process in the unconscious, since it is not brought to the conscious mind for communication purposes. Then the healing force in the unconscious will create new symbols to heal and transform the emotion. Joseph Campbell,* a cross-cultural mythologist, would say this would allow deep mysteries to unfold since it keeps communication at a metaphoric level. The deep self can then shift, change, or heal the emotion without having to be tied down by the conscious mind and the controlling ego.

Emotions are difficult to deal with, not only because of our enculturation and our need to seem a superior, good, or strong person. They are difficult to deal with because of where they are mediated within the physiology of our mind.

The limbic system of the brain regulates emotions. By using imagery, a process which "talks" to the limbic system and which has easy access to the unconscious mind, a person can learn to sense and transform emotions in a profound manner.

Emotions and Primitive Intuition

Working with emotions is not only important to heal suppressed pain and trauma and to meet the esteem needs necessary for transcendence, but it is also important for psychic work. As noted above, imagery and emotions are both regulated by the limbic system in the brain. From research with animals, Karl Pribram* claims that the limbic system is the site of intuition. Animals have a form of primitive intuition tied to emotions. For example, a horse may appear skittish when it senses rain coming.

Emotions and intuition are closely linked in their functioning by the physical site of their activity within the mind.

People often confuse emotions and intuition. They "see" in their psychic visions what they really want to happen. A psychic may see, for example, what he or she wants to happen, instead of what he or she is sensing intuitively. If a person wants to be "clear" in psychic work, then working with emotions is critical.

If you want to work in psychic realms then you need to refine your intuition so that you are not confusing your emotions with psychic information. To develop this refinement, you must undertake the process of releasing emotions buried in the unconscious through acceptance and humility. You need to be able to discriminate between intuitive feelings and emotional feelings. This only happens when the many layers of emotions within the being are re-sensed accurately, accepted, integrated and released.

The Wild Human Animal

A part of people's resistance to working with their emotions is the feeling they must be in control of their emotions to be civilized. Tribal people and animals react instinctually with their emotions. This is seen by our culture as something bad. From this perspective the animal nature must be transcended. This translates to denying emotions that are seen as animal-like. Rage, anger, trust, sensual pleasure, and hurt are emotions to be avoided. But we all have these emotions. To pretend that we don't have them, we will have to suppress them. Of course the list of bad emotions varies by individual history, class, and societal experiences.

Animal nature is seen as a dark force residing in the unconscious, and we treat it as if it doesn't exist. But it does exist, and if it is not valued and integrated, then it will rage out of control in the unconscious and rear its head in counterproductive ways. It takes energy to hold something in the unconscious out of the mind's conscious awareness. Eventually, the mind will need its energy elsewhere and will not be able to keep it suppressed. The suppressed emotions or qualities will come in bursts that can hurt the individual. Even animal-like emotions are integral to our human experience.

Our animal nature is ancient. It holds the mysteries of creation and the centuries of Earth evolution. Oddly, wild animal nature is central to spiritual work—another paradox. The task is to bring the awareness into the animal nature. This makes us whole; spirit manifest in physical form. There is not a dichotomy between the Earth and the spirit. The Earth is spirit. It is all one thing. Lack of integration of our wild animal nature results in people with an enormous part of the mind controlling them in an unconscious way. A person is then truly "out of control," because the conscious mind is walled in from the strong forces of the unconscious. These forces motivate behavior, but the person does not understand the reason for the behavior. Addiction, violence, and depression can result. By integrating the animal nature in the unconscious, we gain strength and stability with the Earth.

Shamans have worked on the Earth for 20,000 years in all cultures. They are spirit travelers who use drumming and the Earth's animal energies to come in contact with the spirit world and bring healing forces to the human community. Today each of us is our own shaman. We travel into our animal nature to find spiritual insights.

How to Work with Emotions

Below are the basic attitudes for working with emotions:

1) Choose to open to whatever is inside of you.

2) Learn to accept any emotion that occurs without judging it, reacting to it, or even figuring out what it means.

3) Stay with an emotion even though you don't like it (i.e., grief, weakness, hurt, depression). You have to stay with an

emotion until you're done with it. Trust your deep self to heal and transform and integrate the emotion. Sometimes this takes a very long time because the emotion has been suppressed for so long.

4) See emotions as signals to patterns, not as feelings to get rid of.

5) Realize you don't need to be "in control" of your emotions. The more you allow yourself to feel, the better off you are.

6) Do not act quickly from your emotions, but feel them, watch them, and sit with them. If you sense an emotion fully, then your intuition will give you insight as to the correct action. It may be expressing the emotion or may not be.

The primary benefit in working with emotions is that the immense amount of mental energy needed to suppress painful emotions or to deny certain kinds of emotions is released. This allows you to open the conscious mind more fully to the unconscious, creating expanded consciousness. You experience the following benefits:

1) Refined intuition;

2) Clarity with psychic experience;

3) Increased energy—energy is released that has been used to trap painful experiences;

4) Wholeness as a human—authenticity with who you are;

5) Feelings of being fully alive—acceptance of the human incarnation;

6) Humility to know that you cannot control or program the emotions that occur within you—acceptance of whatever comes up inside of you and non-conformity to some idealized notion of who you should be.

Emotions are also signals of karmic patterns. This means that when you get a strong emotion about something, it is probably connected to some basic structure in your mind. This structure has been unconsciously developed in this lifetime or in previous ones. By staying with the emotion and sensing it fully, the karmic pattern can be brought to consciousness and then released. An example might be that in a past life, you have acted as a martyr. The sacrificial or martyr reaction to a situation is, therefore, a basic pattern in your struggle with life. Let us say that you go around sacrificing yourself for others. However, you find that it does not help others gain in their awareness. They just seem to use you. You start feeling abused, accompanied by deep feelings of pain and rage. If you stay with these emotions as long as it takes to release them, then you could release the pattern as well. You can then learn to be compassionate to others, but not necessarily to feel compelled to take others' pain. When you get a strong emotion, it's a signal to stay with that emotion to release karmic patterns.

Stages of Emotional Work

There are basic stages people go through with emotional work. These are created through observation of many people proceeding with spiritual work in awareness. There are some commonalities in the progression of this work which could be seen as stages. Some people may skip a stage or be stuck in one stage. People can move up and down through the stages, but there is usually a general progression, over time, sometimes across years, through these stages. These stages can also be seen as applicable to each new emotional wound or dysfunctional personality structure or karmic pattern uncovered in the unconscious. Each time you open to something in the unconscious mind, your conscious mind progresses through these stages in healing the wound or releasing the pattern.

Stage One: Denial

This stage has been well documented above. The basic operating mode is that one should not be emotional, except for a few emotions that are okay depending on one's sex, ethnic heritage, and social milieu. Some new-agers aptly fit this stage. They begin spiritual work with meditation or yoga or attending human potential workshops and open to the spirit within them. Initially there are beautiful empowering feelings of this wonderful force being released. Pretty soon, however, the controlling ego latches on to this phenomenon, and the person adopts values to prove they are superior in their spirituality.

The person in the denial stages focuses on something that separates them from others to fortify their need for superiority. For example, what makes them better could be a specific spiritual practice, a dietary practice, or specific beliefs.

Some Evangelical Christians may also fit the denial stage, since the Holy Spirit working in them creates altered states of expansion at first. Individuals seize on these empowering experiences to make themselves better than others.

Some people stay in this stage, and others proceed because pain begins. Pain occurs when a person realizes that beliefs that they have formed in relationship to their spiritual growth may not be correct. The specific beliefs or practices they have do not always work. For example, a new-ager may not be able to heal his or her physical self through affirmations, or an evangelical may see some non-Christian behaviors in their peers, like racism or abusing others in business matters. Or a budding psychic could do a psychic reading and find out later that the reading was totally incorrect. A blocked colon could be mistaken for a heart condition, for example. When you are using a spiritual system to create psychological superiority, your spiritual system has to be infallible.

However, once you see errors in your system you can use this information to grow further. The funny thing about spiritual work is that you can't hide from it. Ram Dass says once you wake up you can't go back to sleep. You can nap off and on, but once you give the spirit body a space in your awareness it will tap you on the shoulder at regular intervals. One interesting phenomenon is that your karma, or the reaction to your actions, speeds up as you open to the spirit. Initially, you start feeling very empowered. Things start working. For example, you can manifest or psychic abilities start developing. At this point your ego gets into the action and you start feeling superior. Then boom, the reaction to these superior feelings is some sort of a crash. You realize you're not so great after all. It is a beautiful process, because you cannot hide from yourself, and you cannot use your spiritual development for ego needs.

Stage Two: Choice

In this stage, the individuals start realizing that maybe they do not have all the answers. Maybe their religious practices are not absolutely correct. Maybe they need to humble themselves to accept what is, instead of what "should" be.

In this stage, the individual registers intent from the conscious mind to the deep self. The intent is to allow whatever is to unfold. "I choose to let whatever is inside of me to come out."

This choice takes a great deal of courage. It is difficult to surrender to the unknown. It is also difficult to choose to be out of control. Our culture and our training teach us to fake being in control at all times.

However, if we coax our conscious mind to relinquish control, our deep self grows and grows. Once we give space for something to happen by making a small, quiet choice, then it will unfold of its own accord. It seems silly to think something will happen by simply saying, "I choose." But the passive use of will is probably the most powerful force we have at our disposal.

Stage Three: Acceptance

This is a very long stage. In the conscious mind, this seems so easy, to accept one's emotions. But for most people, what emerges from the inside will shake their very core. Feelings that society thinks are bad emerge: jealousy, hatred, pain, scorn and more. Sometimes the feelings are so strong, all that one can do is to sit with the feeling.

The process of working with emotions is always the same. It is similar to a spiritual practice. You experience the emotion fully no matter what it is. You feel it and watch it without reacting. This type of process runs counter to the stereotype of the so-called spiritual person as described in the first of this chapter. That person was always serene and calm, and supposedly in control. But being spiritual is not what you think it is. Gurus from the East are known to play tricks on their devotees by doing things that the devotees think are not in keeping with a spiritual master. Ram Dass' guru took a handful of LSD amidst Ram Dass' protestations. The LSD had no effect. If you think you know what spirituality is, you are on the wrong track.

Accepting yourself is a continual test of your commitment to the spiritual path. This is true because so much will come up that is in opposition to your thoughts of what is good or true. It is important to note that accepting emotions is different than acting on them. If you feel rage you do not hurt someone else, you just sense the emotion completely.

Stage Four: Disintegration

The paradox of the spiritual path is that as you gain in aware-ness you will feel emotions more strongly. You think that you will become calmer, but you find that you are more emo-tional and sensitive. Intense feelings of weakness and leth-argy are common. This makes it seem that you are doing something wrong. As you do your practice of feeling fully and watching, more and more will emerge from your uncon-scious. Childhood traumas come up. Deep feelings of unwor-thiness which may be based on the human race's karma will rear their head. Also, images from the ancient animal evolu-tion of the Earth will come up. You may see yourself become a bat or a giant reptile or a dragon. Sometimes these experi-ences are so vivid that you can see the scales on your belly. You watch it, experience it fully, and do not react with judg-ment.

States of disintegration are quite positive since it means that the structures of your conscious mind are breaking up. These structures were erected to make you feel okay about yourself and possibly superior to others. Disintegration means that these structures are breaking up. Disintegration is good. On the spiritual path all that you thought you were will crash.

You may also have physical sensations of shaking. The Hindu goddess Kali is an apt metaphor for the action that is happening in the emotional body. Kali represents death and destruction, but she also represents regeneration. Dysfunc-tional structures need to be broken before new functional structures can grow. Mother Teresa's first home for the dying was in a former temple to the goddess Kali, an appropriate home for death and transformation. Kali's energy teaches that after destruction of the conscious mind can come the rebirth and emergence of the real self buried in the unconsciousness. Structures must die before the unconscious becomes conscious.

Jean Houston,* a psychologist specializing in imagery, talks about depth charges. As the spiritual body grows, it sends energies into the other bodies of the person, the physical, mental, and emotional. The spiritual body is connected to all other life and as such has access to an enormous amount of energy. As you release karma and trauma from your unconscious, you unleash a great deal of energy. You will receive depth charges through your physical and emotional body as your spiritual body grows into these other bodies. You may also experience psychic breaks. A great deal of psychic or spiritual energy comes through you as your conscious mind releases its hold on reality. A psychic break is an influx of psychic energy so strong that it results in physical disorientation or weakness or confusion.

The best thing to do in this state where you feel confused and out of control and maybe even a little crazy is to stay with the practice. The following guidelines assist with the disintegration stage:

1) Trust your deep self and your intuition.

2) Stay with the moment of experience.

3) Release expectations of yourself. Rest or physical activity can also help.

Stage Five: Disequilibrium

This stage is a continuation of the previous one, but many of the structures of the mind are broken. There is not the feeling of death from the goddess Kali; it is more a state of undifferentiated ambiguity. Again this stage can take a long time. But within this stage is a feeling of peace and bliss. As you give your spirit more space to grow, then you will have strong feelings of being connected to your deep purpose. The dualism that Western culture uses to define reality starts to disappear. You are not exactly sure what is right or wrong. However, your intuition and your heart give you clear signals about right action and purpose. Your mind is confused, and

Figure 9. The ancient Chinese symbol of the Tao.

that is good. However, you may notice you do some things amazingly well. You may notice things coming out of your mouth that sound quite clear and articulate. You may complete a task with precision. It is amazing the power you have when your mind releases its hold on reality. It is the paradox of finding power by letting go of it.

In the previous stage of disintegration, the emotion seemed to take over. In this stage you develop a point of awareness within the emotion. During disequilibrium your awareness increases and you actually become the emotion. Throughout this stage are feelings of weakness and vulnerability alternating with times of peace, bliss, or exhilaration. There is a certain serenity in watching the explosion inside.

A concept from Taoism, an ancient Chinese spiritual tradition, is applicable to this stage. The Tao is an ancient Chinese metaphor for the energies of the universe (see figure 9 above).

One side is dark and the other side is light. All energies can be seen in this opposite manner (i.e., evil and good, joy and pain, young and old). The circle of the Tao teaches us that these energies are really one energy in their essence. Love is close to hate, as pain and bliss have an underlying essence that is one energy. The Tao teaches us the unity of all energy and challenges us to transcend a dualistic, or good and bad explanation of phenomena. Within the framework of the Tao is the idea of the reversal of the Tao. This principle states that when one polarity is embraced fully, then the energy automatically moves into the other pole. If you are out of balance with the Tao and only put your energy into one pole, then you will actually be in the other pole. For example, if you feel you must always be strong and your conscious mind suppresses any perceptions to the contrary, then you will actually be weak from unconscious needs. Another example is that in the U.S. culture, the pole of the rational or scientific is so emphasized that as a society we are doing very irrational things, like destroying the ozone.

In the application of the reversal of the Tao to emotional/ spiritual work, you need to embrace the poles of energy you have avoided in order to achieve balance. For most people in our culture this means moving fully into weakness and vulnerability to be strong.

Stage Six: Humility

This is the stage of realization that life is a continual process of being fully in the moment and letting go. One realizes that the sooner one dies to one's expectations then the sooner the pain one is experiencing will end. One also realizes that there will be many feelings that are out of one's control. There is no end. There is only the process of living. Many things will fall away. The need to achieve in a certain way or the need for having people love you in a certain way will change. It also becomes quite clear to you that if you put yourself above others, it will impede your progress. Karma accelerates so that when you take actions based on feelings of superiority, then you receive an immediate "slap" of some sort. You know you must surrender to the process whatever that brings. All you have is the moment of your experience and the awareness you bring to it.

This is accompanied by great sublime feelings of ecstasy, peace, and bliss. You are not sure what you know or what you will do, but you are continually surrendering to the universe and the compassion of the universe. You actually feel what it means to say the Buddha's heart is everywhere. There is great strength in the passive receptivity of your own being.

The humility stage brings the person a certain level of stability in being and awareness, although previous stages (i.e., denial and disintegration) are returned to as deeper levels in the unconscious are released. A person learns to move through these stages more quickly, though the process will always take one by surprise.

Stage Seven: Subtleness

A person moves into a more peaceful stage in which the ups and downs are not so high or low. In addition, disintegrative experiences, although difficult, become a normal part of existence. The conscious mind has been dismembered. There is greater trust in the deep self to guide behavior, even though reality appears confused at times. Synchronicity increases. There is also a softness about the person's being and energy.

Sexuality

No chapter on emotions is complete without a discussion of sexuality. Desire is a very strong emotion. As other emotions become exaggerated or intensified in the spiritual practice, so does sexual desire. In fact this emotion may become more exaggerated than the others because sexual orgasm is the closest feeling to the spiritual feeling of unity.

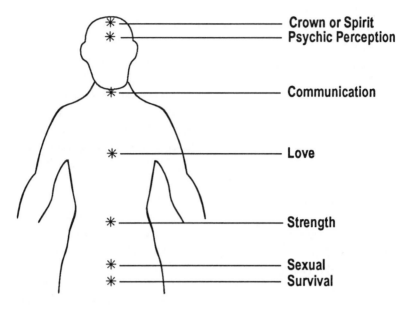

Figure 10. The seven chakras.

Hindu thought may help explain this with the concept of energy centers in the body or chakras. Chakra means wheel in Sanskrit. A chakra takes in and also produces energy. There are seven chakras. The chakras go up the spine (see figure 10 above).

The bottom chakra corresponds with survival needs, the second deals with sexual or procreative needs, the third is for physical strength, the fourth mediates love, and the fifth has to do with communication. The sixth is the psychic third eye, and the seventh is the crown or spiritual chakra. Maslow may have used the chakra system in creating his need hierarchy.

The chakra of interest here is the sexual chakra. Many times on the spiritual path if one is doing intense spiritual practice, this chakra will open and intense sexual energy will be released. Hindu thought also contains the concept of the

Kundalini energy, or a coiled serpent at the base of the spine. This is the creative energy of the spiritual body. With spiritual practice, the Kundalini can rise with an enormous surge of energy. Certain members of the Sikh religion in the United States wear turbans which are, in part, designed to prevent Kundalini overloads by keeping the Kundalini energy from escaping the head. This energy may be what is released during depth charges or psychic breaks. If you have a spiritual practice you can deal with these charges by keeping a focus of attention while the surges occur.

The strong sexual urge accompanying the opening of the spirit is often a surprise because of the common Western notion that you are supposed to become somewhat inhuman and rise above base human emotions as you become spiritual. What do you do here? Do you suppress them? Do you act on them like the Zen master in San Francisco who slept with his students? The way to deal with intense sexual desire is the same process as dealing with other emotions. You sense the emotion completely without acting on it. Insight on what to do with the emotion will come in time. It is important not to act on it impulsively. You know that if you act out of what you desire you may create more pain for yourself. Therefore the task is to treat your desire carefully, making sure you watch and sense the emotion completely. You let go of the outcome of your desire and wait for insight. It is critical not to deny it or suppress these feelings, because sexual energy is a metaphor for surrendering oneself into the whole of awareness. The point here is not to act on sexual desire, but to sense the emotion completely until you have insight on what to do about it. Don't act, don't suppress, don't deny, but sense.

Imagery Exercise: Transforming Emotions

These exercises are not a panacea. They will not fix people. But the deep mysteries and the healing force in each person is contacted by creating metaphors of pain and transforming these metaphors. This has the power to heal.

Think about a scene in the last few weeks in which you had an emotion that you did not like.

Play the scene in your mind as if it is happening now. Where are you? Notice some detail about where you are. This could be something on a table, or a leaf on a tree if you are outside. What colors and sounds do you notice?

Who is in the scene with you? Notice some detail about what another person is wearing? What does this person's face look like?

What is happening in the scene? Who is saying what? Let the scene roll just like you are watching or acting in a movie.

Now let the scene complete itself.

Where in your body do you feel the emotion from the scene? Do not name this feeling. Just go to your body where you are feeling something. Is it in your stomach, your heart, your chest, your head? Where is it?

How big is this feeling? How big a space inside your body does it take up? What are its dimensions?

Now if you could symbolize this emotion, what would it look like? It can either be a physiological symbol or a metaphor for what the feeling might mean. Go to the place where you are feeling something and make a symbol of what it would look like. Again notice details. What color is the symbol? What is the texture? As in previous exercises, if you see a vague form or color, just keep watching this until it becomes more in focus.

At this point give yourself permission to change the symbol of the emotion. What do you want to do with it? Change it. Take it out. Wrap it up. You can do anything in your imagination. Give yourself time with this. Keep returning to the symbol and seeing what you want to do with it. Then let the shift complete itself. Return to the place in your body where you initially felt something. How does it feel now?

Imagery Story: Jill and the Black Dot of Pain

Jill was in a deep depression. She had a bipolar disorder or serious and sudden mood swings from elated highs to deep depression. When she was depressed, it was very difficult to function. She was on medication, but it didn't really help with the feelings of unworthiness she had. She *hated* herself when she was depressed. What good was she to anyone, particularly herself? It was the type of depression where there is no hope.

The feeling was in her heart. It was very heavy and black. It took up a big space in her heart. It felt like it was the entire Earth and it was coated with black. She said she had coated the Earth with black in her heart to take away the great pain of the world.

She could shrink the black sphere to a very tiny dot. This took a long time. When she shrank the Earth down to a dot it moved out of her heart.

She could pick up the dot with her fingers and hold it out. She actually moved her hand out and held her thumb and index finger together. After a very long time she could release the black dot and throw it up. She didn't want to because then people would hurt. But she wasn't really helping people by holding on to this pain. She released the dot with sadness and joy.

Chapter Five

Psychic Stuff

I was living in Coos Bay, Oregon and had traveled to Eugene to hear Buckminister Fuller talk. He was very old then. He leaned to one side, and his glasses were so thick he almost seemed blind. He talked about how he found his calling. He had decided that he wanted to achieve one thing that would help the most people out, so he created cheap shelters for humans with the geodesic dome.

After I returned home, it seemed as if I had received *darshan* or a blessing from an enlightened master. I actually felt an opening in my consciousness. It was a physical sensation of the right side of my mind opening, like a radius of an angle opening.

At the same time, I had found a little book at a raw food bookstore in Portland; the book was called *Space Channeling*.[1] I read it, and it told me how to channel for spirits. It was scary to me, because I had the strong sense that I could do it. Even though scared, some part of me pursued it.

I started channeling by meditating and then writing questions and answers. It wasn't really automatic writing. However, I was in an altered state, like when in deep relaxation after yoga practice. The answers that I wrote down were things that I would not have thought of.

---

[1]Sundar, *Space Channeling*. (Santa Cruz, CA: Rainbow Bridge Construction, 1976).

After awhile I didn't need to meditate or write. I would just ask a question in my mind and get an answer. The entity I channeled for said his name was Deva Lama, and he definitely had a sense of humor. He would give me koan-like answers to simple questions. For example, I asked where I was going to move, and he said, "Your home is in your heart."

Deva had many lessons for my ego. One had to do with ego-tripping on emotions. At an earlier time in my life I had enjoyed playing with existential terror. I would wake up in the night and think that after I died I would not even know that I had lived. I would then get terrified and walk around shaking in a state of panic.

One night, after I started channeling for Deva Lama, I started thinking about death and experiencing that fear. Deva appeared in my mind and started laughing hysterically at me. He said, "It's just your ego that is afraid; you're not."

What is the Psychic World?

Psychic perception is a special form of intuition. Sometimes a person uses intuition to know the direction to turn when driving to a certain destination. This is not an example of psychic perception since it deals with material reality (i.e., the physical location of where you want to go).

However, if you are out in the woods sitting under a tree, and you get a vision of a wolf coming to you, this vision may seem like it is coming from a different reality. This may be psychic perception, since it is intuition applied to a nonmaterial reality.

Being psychic is an extension of being intuitive; it is just a different medium. In one case, the medium is physical reality, and in the other, it is the spirit world or nonmaterial reality. The basic point is that being intuitive and being psychic are both perceptive-like processes. You sense something, or in new-age terms, you "get" something.

Multiple realities exist, and the process of sensing psychic phenomena can be applied to those realities that are nonmaterial or subtle in nature. A non-dualistic realm of multiple realities presents itself when you enter the spirit world. Psychic phenomena can be seen as a subset of various realities that are spiritual or nonmaterial in nature.

Thinking of multiple realities as energy levels may serve as a useful model. For example, the levels of energy could include physical, mental, emotional and, finally, spiritual levels. The first and second levels could be perceived by our physical senses, with intellectual energy being an abstraction of physical reality. Emotions, as the next level, could be best perceived through the body-sense of primitive intuition. Then the spiritual level could be best perceived through a psychic perception.

As Einstein has taught us, energy and matter are interchangeable. For example, a particle can be seen as a point or a wave. Both realities exist simultaneously. It depends on the instruments that are used to examine the phenomenon. It may be possible to extend this idea to propose different levels of energy for different levels of reality. Energy levels of consciousness are found in Hindu philosophy and have been used by a number of writers including Ken Wilber. The wavelength of different colors provides a simple metaphor for understanding these energy levels. Each color has a different wave length. Red has the longest wave length, orange's wavelength is a little shorter, moving up to purple being the shortest. Similarly, material reality or the body may be likened to red and is a very concrete reality. The next level of energy may be emotions which is less concrete in nature. These levels continue to progress as they become less dense to other levels that are nonmaterial in nature. These are the multiple realities of the spirit world.

Different energy levels require different modes of perception. Some levels of energy can be perceived through the physical senses, others through the intuitive senses. And other levels are perceived through the more refined or subtle psychic sense. Psychic perception is the way to sense the reality of spirit worlds.

A non-dualistic reality model is very difficult for the Western mind to apprehend. Our culture teaches very clear rules through the scientific tradition for determining what is real and what is not real. This unconscious tendency of determining what is real and unreal must be relearned to work with nonmaterial levels of reality. In order to experience other realities, a person is forced to suspend judgment of determining what is true and not true. At the same time the mind must be focused, so that a person's strong reactions (i.e.fear) to psychic events will not overtake the event. With focused attention, a person can feel a strong emotion without reacting to it. These elements of suspending judgment and focusing the mind are necessary for a person to allow vivid visionary experiences to happen even when they are accompanied by major physical and emotional responses.

What About Psychic Murky Zones?

A lot of people who work psychically will protect themselves from negative energy by surrounding themselves with white light or even creating mirrors that reflect negative energy back to the sender. This brings up the topic of whether there are good or bad kinds of psychic energy. To transcend dualism once again, the question may be more aptly framed to ask whether or not different levels of psychic energy have different effects. Certainly the answer to this question is "Yes!"

There are dark or murky levels of energy. The *Tibetan Book of the Dead* describes some of these realms. After you die the first realm that you pass through might be described as a murky zone. If you have trained your attention through meditation or some other practice, you can then focus on a white light when it appears in this zone. By paying attention to the light you move through the murk. The murky zone seems to occupy an energy level between material and non-material reality.

What is this murky psychic world? It could be spirits who are caught and cannot reincarnate. They then hang out at the transition between matter and spirit. It could even be karmic debris. No one can say what this energy is. The point is that there are certain realities that contain energy that serves to cloud or twist one's psychic perception. Usually working in this realm exaggerates one's deepest fears.

Yoga tradition teaches that as a person becomes more and more adept at practicing yoga or disciplining the attention, the person becomes more psychic. From a yoga standpoint the person is then able to work with the subtle force of prana. The term *prana* in Hindu philosophy is defined as that nonmaterial essence which manifests into the material forms. Many people think that prana is breath. It is true that one of the limbs or practices of yoga is *pranayama* which includes breath exercises. However, prana is the force underlying the breath, not the breath itself. Prana is more aptly understood as life force, or the subtle energy that pervades all life and holds the universe together.

Using the energy level model, prana or the subtle force would be at an upper level. This is a very powerful level. Since this energy level is so strong, it is best to take care. Even though yoga practice will help a person become more psychic, yoga teaches a practitioner not to pursue psychic awareness in and of itself. This teaching is designed to keep yogis on the path to enlightenment and not to be turned by the seductiveness of psychic knowledge. To prevent this, the yogi watches the psychic experiences, but does not give energy to them. In other words, if a person keeps a focus and a detachment during psychic experiences, then the person will not get lost in the murky zone.

Psychic Information as Symbolic and Metaphoric

It is important to note that perceptions from these various levels of energy come in metaphors. A person does not get a logical treatise from a nonmaterial reality. Symbols come, pictures or visions emerge, and these then are screened through the rational mind which tries to imbue meaning to these symbols. Often the symbols are unique to an individual's background. Therefore it appears that psychic information differs across people and cultures. But at a deeper level the symbolic meaning itself may be constant.

People that "die"—cease breathing, end brain activity, and then resume those functions—report after-life experiences that correspond with their personal beliefs of what happens after death. These after-life experiences occur as visions or images. The people "experience" events. Christians often see Christ welcoming them and see relatives who have already died. Hindus see Krishna greeting them and see the multitudes of souls awaiting incarnation. These visions are symbols of the event and not necessarily literal, logical stories of what is happening.

People who start to become psychic often apply a dualistic construct to their experiences. They try to be correct and accurately predict what is going to happen on the physical plane. The fact is that people cannot be right psychically, they can only sense a perception. Therefore the best way to process psychic information that you sense or that you may receive from someone else is to see how the information feels to you. Does this information resonate with your body sense and your intuition? It is wise to be wary of psychic information that is very specific in content. For example, if a channeler tells you that you are having troubles with your mate, because you and he were brother and sister in past incarnations, this should not be taken as literal truth.

The correct stance to psychic phenomena is to treat them with meditative attention—to watch and to not react, but to wait for insight on the meaning as you trust the body reaction.

Psychic Perception and Emotions

As you experience other levels of energy, you actually live them. In addition, you feel the emotions as if these events are actually happening. I have often experienced other's emotions as I am reading someone's aura, particularly as a tragic event from childhood emerges. I will cry as I re-experience this event by interacting with the person's aura. This emotion does not stay with me, for it is not mine. However, when I perceive the event psychically, I experience the emotion involved with the event as well. This is similar to empathy in counseling.

Emotions are truly central to psychic work and are often ignored by people who write about spiritual development. Emotions are markers of karmic patterns that need to be cleared for accurate psychic perception. Emotions are messages from the body's primitive intuition. They are more accurate perceptions of reality than what is in the mind. Emotions are the carriers of peak altered-state experiences because they create bliss and peace. Emotions seem to be directly tied to neuropeptide production, which in turn affects immune activity and the body's state of health. By learning to clearly sense emotions within the body, a person can train his or her intuition and bypass the interference of the mind. Imaging emotions in the body can be a path to clarity of perception. You cannot deny emotions and become psychic; you will only become delusionary. Working with the emotions is a prerequisite to working in multiple realities.

The fact that emotions and intuition are so closely linked adds to the importance of treating psychic experiences from a meditative stance. This means to experience them fully, but to suspend judgment. Psychic perceptions come from multiple energy levels, are symbolic and transrational in nature, and are closely tied to the emotions. Therefore they are a phenomenon to be treated with respect and care.

Psychic Perception and the Ego

The primary issue with psychic phenomena is the same as with all issues of spiritual development. It comes down to one word, and that word is *control*. Are you going to try to gain personal power by controlling your psychic perceptions or are you going to allow your psychic perceptions to come?

Many people get enamored with their psychic perceptions. The ego rears its head, as if it has found a commodity for use in gaining superiority over others. Also it is fun to be psychic; to tell people things that no one else knows and to be correct on future events or pinpointing someone's physical problem. But the problem is that most psychics are not always right, and they do not necessarily know whether they are right or wrong. Remember psychic perception is a form of intuition and as such is like any perception. It is subject to unconscious screening by the individual. The following story shows how playing with the psychic world can contain some hard lessons.

Sandy was one of my students. She was very psychic, and she enjoyed it, in part. Sandy could make people look at her. She would focus on someone across the room and start nudging them psychically. One day she came up to me and said that she wanted to work on me. She had seen a vision the night before in which an old man with a sickle was standing behind my back. Sandy was very dramatic in describing what she saw. I knew Sandy and thought that she was lost in the murky zones and that she had not cleared her ego from her psychic work. But I always figure that to clear my own ego I need to listen to what someone else has to say about me and not assume that my perception is more valid. I try to stay humble, because I know what karma is like when it slaps me in the face.

Sandy wanted to work on me psychically, so I let her. My belief is not to put mirrors or white light around me to protect me but to create a totally empty space within myself. I keep my attention by using this emptiness. This is quite difficult at times, especially when someone is pushing you around psychically. I could feel lots of energy coming from her as she worked on me. She also kept seeing a lot of dark things in my stomach. It was a bit difficult to stay with my emptiness. She saw a dark old man behind my shoulder. After awhile, Sandy became terrified of me and would not come near me for many days. I had reflected back her psychic energy which she was trying to use to control me. And it was scary to her.

Sandy saw her fears in my aura. It could be that she was accurate in her psychic perception of certain metaphors for me to pay attention to. But the problem was her attempts at control through her psychic will. As noted before, as you progress on your spiritual path, karma speeds up. Reaction to your actions that are motivated by the ego comes fast and furious. The acceleration of karma may be because a person is working on a more subtle level of energy. As yogis teach us, changes in the subtle realm create changes in the material universe. Therefore when people are working with subtle forms of energy, the effects of their actions will be stronger. This is opposed to working in a material reality which carries with it a delay of the reaction. It is best to take care, to go slow, and to not assume that you or someone else is correct psychically. Sharing perceptions is a better strategy. It is wise to remove oneself as the agent of the psychic energy and to watch it.

How Do You Become Psychic?

The primary way that one becomes psychic is the same way that one becomes intuitive. *You clear a space in the mind.* This allows the deep self to surface and provide insights. The deep self is connected to multiple realities, some of which occupy a dimension not bound by time and space. Therefore as an individual becomes more open, that person surrenders the conscious mind's control of reality and unifies with the deep self. This allows the person to sense information from other wavelengths, some of them psychic.

You become psychic by practice and discipline. This is one of those paradoxes that abound in spiritual work. The way to chart multiple realities, which are amorphous and difficult to define, is to refine the attention of the mind. The will of the mind is honed so that it can contain nothing. And by containing nothing it contains all forms of reality. The intent of the practice is important: to surrender to what is, as opposed to gaining control.

Practice—practice is the way. But another paradox presents itself. To develop psychic awareness, one must not try hard to focus and discipline the mind. Instead, one must learn to control the will so that the mind can relax as a focus is held. There is much written about spiritual practice by many authors. The reader can choose a practice as he or she listens to the body sense and inner voice of the intuition. The imagery work in this book can also be a practice. One suggested in Chapter Three is to use the body sense to find an emotion and to then focus on the place in the body to see an image of the emotion. This allows a person to fine tune the attention by keeping it focused on a certain point.

It is true that some people appear to be psychic without this practice. These people almost seem to be born psychic. They have vivid imagery experiences from a young age and see things that other people do not. They too can benefit from a practice that disciplines the attention. This will clear the ego from their work and make their perceptions clearer.

Oracles

There is a lot of oracle work these days. Mainstream society looks at it with some distaste and judgment. Look at the heat former president Reagan received when it became public that he listened to his wife's astrologer. Basically oracle work is creating answers about future events, a psychic process. Some common oracles include channelers, the *I Ching*, tarot cards, and aura readers. There are many more, but these are presented as examples. However, the cautions and guidelines for using this type of psychic information are the same, as you will discover.

Channeling is when a person speaks for a spirit. One book, *Seth Speaks*,[2] is the channeling example that has been around for the longest period of time. Some channelers can speak for more than one spirit. Some seem to go into a trance or be taken over by the spirit. Sometimes channelers like Ramtha have people that follow them as spiritual teachers.

The tendency of some people is to invest the channeler with an authority or expert status. This is a mistake. The main thing to use as a check in working with a channeler is to keep track of your own body sense to the person's information and to trust this body reaction, more than the channeler. Also it is wise to pick and choose from the channeled information and use specific information as metaphors or symbols.

The *I Ching Book of Changes* is an ancient Chinese Taoist oracle that is based on the concept that change in any phenomenon affects all other parts of existence synchronistically. If people can learn to perceive changes in cosmic energy, then they can open themselves to unite with these energies, thereby creating harmony. Either sticks or coins are thrown. Then the pattern of the coins or sticks determines whether a line is drawn, either closed or broken. The coins

---

[2]Roberts, J. *Seth Speaks: The Eternal Validity of the Soul*. (*New York: Prentice Hall Press, 1972*).

are thrown six times, creating a pattern of six lines or a hexagram, which is made up of two sets of three lines each. Each of these lines can be changing. There are 64 hexagrams and each has a word and a story, which is often interpreted for the reader. Danger, Nourishing, Innocence, Repeating and Moderation are examples of hexagrams. When a given hexagram is thrown, it is examined for advice. The *I Ching* is a very powerful tool and it is difficult to make it conform to one's desires by pushing it around psychically. There is a mystery in the metaphors used which baffles the conscious mind, but speaks to the deep self. Therefore it is a very reliable oracle.

The *tarot* is a deck of cards. There are many tarot decks, but in general they contain four suits of cards, similar to a playing deck. The different suits signify different energies. For example, a given deck may have the suits of The World (material reality), Crystals (mental forces), Wands (energy), and Cups (emotions). The numbers of cards also convey different energies; for example, threes convey synthesis and fives convey struggle.

In addition to cards that are in a suit, or the Minor Arcana, there are other cards that convey more definitive forces. These are called the Major Arcana.

Tarot used to be seen as "dark" and was used by people to control psychic energy. But there are many decks now that are designed to reflect, not control energies. Supposedly long ago the ancients got together to decide how to convey the mysteries now contained in tarot. They concluded that if they put them in a book, no one would read it, but if they were put in a game, they would continue. Some say the tarot is based on the ancient Kabbalah. The tarot is fun. However, it is a bit addictive and, at times, can be manipulated psychically to conform to a person's desires. It is best to keep a respectful attitude, or else not to take it too seriously.

Aura Reading occurs when a person psychically examines the nonmaterial energy body of another person. Some psychics visually see auras and others feel auras. It seems that psychics have certain gifts. For example, some are great at finding physical ailments, while others seem to know the exact time when someone will die. Aura reading is interesting stuff, but the same advice applies as for channelers. Trust the body sense more than the psychic.

Oracles can be looked at as tools to understand subtle energies which will affect life in the future. Another way of looking at them is as rituals to trick the conscious mind into letting go, so that a person's deep self can talk through symbols. There are some things to keep in mind when working with oracles:

1) Don't look for answers outside yourself. Trust your deep self.

2) Be particularly wary of psychic information that gives you a lot of specifics about the future. Remember psychic sensations are nonverbal in nature. Therefore the person interprets the psychic information through his or her emotions, desires, and perceptions.

3) Trust your body sensation to the information. Does it feel right? Does it resonate with something inside you?

4) Suspend judgment as you listen to the psychic information. Don't assume it is right or wrong. Just let it in. Then wait for insight about what to do with the information.

5) Don't be intimidated or pushed around psychically. Hold your attention, keep your heart and mind empty, and watch and feel what is going on. Don't be afraid to push someone out of your space if it doesn't feel good. Never give your power away, but don't use it to control the other person either.

Summary

Psychic awareness is fun, and multiple realities are a great playground to experiment in and learn about other dimensions. But there are definite dangers to the naive psychic traveler. Psychic work will eventually come to you if you are serious about your spiritual development. As you clear your mind and surrender your control, you naturally start moving into more subtle realms of energy.

Be wise by not trying to gain power in psychic work. Just keep it as another form of seeing, maybe correct and maybe not. Don't be afraid of multiple realities. You will learn that there is more "truth" to moving in and out of realities than in holding on to the concrete material world. The wonders of the spirit world are truly magnificent. But you may face terrors and be shaken to your core. So take care, arm yourself with the purity of your spiritual practice and the intent of your will to be one with the universal forces of compassion.

Imagery Exercise: Power Animal

In shamanic tradition, each animal has a specific way, often called a medicine way. The shaman in a vision would travel to the underworld and bring back a power animal that would help a patient's sickness or imbalance. The power animal with its special animal medicine would then be breathed into the patient.

Imagery is the vehicle that allows us to journey and receive healing information for ourselves. Animals are excellent symbols to use for imagery, since their animate qualities prompt movement in the image. Remember when images move of their own accord, it means that the underlying matrix of the mind or the deep self is operating and directing the images. An animal can symbolize a quality hidden within that could be helpful at this time. For example, an eagle can symbolize vision or insight and a bear can symbolize courage. It is best not to have a preconception of what the animal in your image signifies. It is much better to wait for an animal and to notice your body sense as a result of interacting with that animal.

Working with animals in images can be helpful and significant. Animal images can also bring down the dualities that the conscious mind is usually locked up in, since certain animals are good and certain animals are bad to people. A deer might be a good image to a person, while a toad is not. Therefore, if a toad came to the person in an image the person would try to make it into something else. But learning to be with the image, whatever it is, helps break dualistic structures in the mind. Who knows, the toad may represent the ability to jump out of hot water when the time is right.

Take a position that feels comfortable. Take your attention into your body. Slowly with intention, gradually with compassion, slow your body down. Carefully take your attention to the places where your body is in contact with a chair, couch, or floor. Psychically stretch out the skin of your body that is in contact with the chair or floor. Move your attention slowly to each part of your body that is in contact. Your feet, the top of your shoulders, your upper arms—feel your whole body becoming flatter and heavier. It is as if your body is sinking into the floor or chair. You are no longer holding the weight of your body up. The weight of your body is naturally moving into a relaxed position. The muscles are releasing the bones and joints.

Relax your feet, your ankles, your calves, your knees, and your thighs. Now move into your abdomen region. Go deep into your body and relax your stomach, colon, pancreas, and liver. Relax your heart muscle. Spend some time here. Think about how smooth and strong it is. Think about the four chambers and valves. Think about how many times it beats a minute. Caress your heart and give it thanks.

Relax your neck, particularly the back part. Open your shoulder joints, first your right and then your left. Release the pressure on the back of your neck. Relax the back of your head, the top of your head, and your ears. Let your eyeballs become heavy and fall to the back of your head. Unlock your jaw. Relax your tongue and lips. Relax your arms and hands. Feel your whole body slowing down.

See yourself outside in a setting that you like, where you have been before. Usually when you are in this setting you feel a certain level of comfort or security. You are able to let go of the cares and troubles of your daily life.

You are walking in this setting and you are feeling it is a good day. Nothing is particularly troubling you. Everything else seems far away, except for the moment of this experience.

Start paying attention to your perceptions of the scene you have created. As you walk, notice the sensation of the ground under your feet. How do your feet feel as they move? Reach out and touch a leaf. Notice the feel of its texture and the color of the leaf. Is it rough or smooth? What do the veins in the leaf look like? You may feel a bush brush across your legs or arms as you walk. Look up. What color is the sky? Are there clouds? Is there a wind against your cheek?

As you walk along, you notice sounds. A bird might sing, or the wind may rustle leaves. Soon you find a place that feels good to you to sit down. You sit down and start attending to the details of the place around you.

After a time, you notice a movement to one side. You have a sense that an animal is coming to see you. You also know that it will not hurt you. Pretty soon the animal comes to you. Now let the image move of its own accord. The animal may talk to you or touch you. Try to notice detail about the animal's color, fur, skin, or feathers. Just stay with the image of the animal for a short while and let it move of its own accord. You can try to make the imagery more vivid by focusing in on a detail like a color or by looking at a form until a piece of it comes into focus. Just keep looking. You may see something as if you are looking into a fog. As the fog moves in and out you get glimpses of an object. You keep looking at the place where you have seen the glimpses so that piece of the image comes more and more into focus.

Stay with the image as long as it feels comfortable. Now let the image complete itself.

Let the image fade, but keep a sense of it, possibly a feeling somewhere in your body. You might want to name that sense or you might just want to be with it. Or you might want to draw it or paint it.

Imagery Story: Connie's Anger

Connie had been committed to spiritual work for several years. She took a trip to Nepal and Tibet and she had passed through the first stage of spiritual development. In this stage, the individual is involved in some sort of spiritual exploration, such as meditation, affirmations, or the *Course in Miracles.* This experimentation brings highs. In this stage, labeled "Denial" in Chapter Two, the conscious mind is still using the desire for spiritual development as a way to be right or good. This also compensates for any deficits a person may have psychologically, like poor self-esteem or abandonment by a parent. In any case, Connie had passed through this first stage and had begun the serious work of staying with the moment of her experience; she was letting go of her notions about the way spiritual work was supposed to go. She was in a disintegration stage, with lots of vulnerable feelings. She also had psychic surges that left her spinning. A lot of issues about her mother were presenting themselves.

I was doing an imagery exercise with her about her mother. Connie was visualizing a scene in her mother's bedroom. Her baby sister had just been born and her mother was fussing over the sister. Connie was in the corner, and no one would notice her. She wanted to hurt her sister in the image, like stick an object in her mouth so that she would choke, but she knew her mother would ignore her more. There seemed no course of action in the image to resolve her anger. She finally grew very big in the image. She was a giant and could look down and see the room with the two figures, as if it were a dollhouse. She then felt that she could send her mother and sister far from her view, because she didn't feel anger any more. It had happened that she was rejected, but she could let go of the role of the hurt child. This role had helped her be strong, but she didn't need it any more. The image then shifted to her as a child standing alone on a hill, screaming at the sky. Connie didn't like her little girl image and wanted her to die.

After several sessions of working with her little girl, the child on the hill begin crying and wasn't angry any more. Connie picked her up and moved her into her heart.

○   ○   ○

It can seem glamorous to work with psychic phenomena, but for the person serious about spiritual growth, it is nothing to take pride in. For no matter how psychic you are, you still must integrate and surrender to your humanity. The path is through your human emotions, body, mind, and spirit, not above them.

Chapter Six

Terrors and Demons

I was sitting meditating in my bedroom. There is an oak floor in my bedroom, and the Buddha that I meditate with is the same color as the oak floor. I had the sensation of smoothness, of tan, polished wood, and of natural tones. Recently, I had been having a lot of psychic breaks, overwhelming rushes of psychic energy charging through my body. I was doing an okay job of staying with the sensations. They were hard though, and I was tired of them. I had a tendency to think that there was something wrong with me when they happened. But after a few negative thoughts, I would bring myself back to staying with the experience, not judging it and trusting my process. One reason I hated psychic breaks was you could never get anything done. It was hard to cook or clean or even get to work.

I was meditating and this big surge came. It was overpowering, but I was not bothered by it this time. I just sat and watched and experienced it. All of a sudden the floor opened up in front of me, down to the ground. The bedroom is on the second story so this is a long distance. This giant serpent came out of the ground. All I could see was the round body which had yellows, tans, and greens. The belly was very shiny, almost iridescent. In this vision I looked down and my body had become the serpent's body. I had become this very long snake-like creature. My belly was scaly but it was nice and soft. I liked the skin, even though on another level it was very repulsive and frightening. I ignored dualistic thoughts that this must be a very bad image. In Christianity serpents are evil, but in North American and Asian traditions snakes are sacred. I was so huge, though, it was hard not to be revolted and terrified.

As the snake I grew bigger and bigger, I broke through the ceiling and was twice as big as the house. Then it was over.

The Hindu goddess Kali signifies death and destruction and people at times see her as bad, evil, or negative. But Kali is also the symbol of rebirth. After structures are destroyed then new forms grow, just as when the snake sheds its skin a new skin grows. Kali symbolizes eternal time. She has stripped off the veils of existence and illusion. Her only garment is space.

Shamanism and the Underworld

Shamanism is a spiritual practice that has been on the planet for a long time. There were shamans practicing in most societies around the Earth 10,000 to 20,000 years ago.

A shaman is the defender of the psychic integrity of a community, according to Mircea Eliade,* author of *Shamanism: Archaic Techniques of Ecstasy*. The shaman "defends life, health, fertility, the world of 'light' against death, diseases, sterility, disaster, and the world of darkness."[1]

The shaman is a specialist in the sacred and travels to the sky world to meet the gods and also descends into the underworld to work with the powers of death and destruction. In the shamanic view of the world, there are three basic

---

[1] Eliade, M. *Shamanism: Archaic Techniques of Ecstasy*. Princeton, N.J.: Princeton University Press, 1964).

cosmic zones—the sky, the Earth, and the underworld, which are linked together along a central axis. The axis provides an opening or a hole for the shaman to move between these cosmic worlds. This axis is sometimes represented as the tree of life, with the roots in the underworld and the branches reaching for the sky.

As Michael Harner* documents in his "how-to" shaman's guide, *The Way of the Shaman*,[2] shamans use various techniques to make these travels. These techniques include herbs that are hallucinogenic, drumming, chants, and ritual. It is of great importance to note that the worlds that shamans experience are very real to them. They are not hallucinating or creating imaginary visions. From a psychological point of view, the physiology that accompanies vivid imagery experiences supports the view that these are actual experiences. In multi-sensory imagery, the body reacts as if the image is actually happening. Additionally, since imagery experiences access the unconscious or the deep structure of the persona, experiences during imagery actually will shift deep structure and lead to changes in the conscious mind. Finally the deep self in the unconscious when accessed with imagery can travel in multiple realities that may be as real as the material reality.

Joan Halifax* in *Shamanic Voices*[3] explains how a person becomes a shaman. A person does not answer an ad in the newspaper, nor are there shaman recruiters at job fairs. One is usually called, through strong visionary experiences. These experiences are so overpowering that the person cannot deny them, but must follow their teaching.

The shaman has been called a light-carrier by some, or we could call this person a light warrior—a person who travels into the unknown to bring back healing gifts to others.

---

[2] Harner, M. *The Way of the Shaman*. (New York: Bantam Books, 1982).
[3] Halifax, J. *Shamanic Voices: A Survey of Visionary Narratives* (New York : E.P. Dutton, 1979).

Often, the shaman drums or someone else drums to access an expanded state of consciousness.

From Chapter Three, it is clear that the rhythmic stimulation activates limbic system activity, opening the doors of the unconscious and possibly stimulating endorphic release to create an ecstatic state. In *The Way of the Shaman,* Harner gives step-by-step instructions on what to achieve and how to travel in a shamanic state of consciousness. In Harner's version, the person looks for a cave or hole to enter in the underworld. After entering the underworld, the person looks for an animal to bring back. Sometimes this animal is called a power animal, and people will have different power animals at any given time depending on the medicine way that is needed. Practices differ greatly across cultures, but the journeying in other realities is a commonality, as is rhythmic stimulation in chanting or drumming, in order to achieve this state.

The shamanic paradigm can have great benefits for those interested in expanded consciousness. First the technique of using drumming to vivify the imagery experience is very effective. It should be noted that most people working with core shamanism, or common qualities across various shamanic traditions, do not advocate the use of drugs for achieving these states. I agree with this recommendation. Drums are as effective and do not have physical side effects or addictive properties. As Ram Dass said, when you use drugs to achieve highs you keep coming back down. In addition hallucinatory drugs seem to enhance perception at first, and then appear to dull it over time.

Another helpful aspect of shamanism is that there are multiple realities. Shamanism proposes three levels, but in all probability there are many more. An additional helpful teaching from shamanism is the view of the underworld, since shamanism is an Earth integrated spiritual tradition. A person can travel to the underworld and interact with animal spirits, some of which are helpers and some of which are "demon-like." The shaman can face the demons without becoming one and without being destroyed. Animals and the Earth hold great mysteries for humans which will bring them healing. One interpretation of journeying to the underworld, is that you must experience dark to become light. Experiences in the underworld can be terrifying indeed. But through these experiences one can gain medicine ways of power to heal oneself and others. Shamanism is presented as a model for a person to use in taking a spirit world journey within the self and traveling in multiple realities. Shamanism is one explanation for psychic phenomena.

Karmic Debris

Karmic debris, located in a person's aura, has accumulated over many incarnations, inherited from a person's individual lineage and also from the entire human lineage. Karmic debris can be seen as residual energy that is stored as a reaction to certain actions and is trapped in the aura. When a person opens a space in the mind through focusing the attention, then issues start emerging from the unconscious. First it appears as psychological issues from the current incarnation. These issues are assumptions that people made early in life about who they were. In addition, traumatic memories emerge that have been suppressed without healing.

The sensations of having these issues emerge from the unconscious may be likened to a whirlpool bringing matter up from the depths. There is a dizzying feeling as the issues arise, spiraling out. Swami Rama,* a spiritual teacher trained in philosophy, psychology and medicine, uses the following phrase for this emergence: "the chitta unwinds." In Hindu philosophy the translation of *chitta* is formless mind stuff. In other words, the mind stuff in the unconscious emerges into the conscious to be released.

Psychological issues of this incarnation are unwound. These issues can present themselves over a long period of time off and on, before they are integrated and released. It is a great test of the will to watch the issues present themselves and to experience them without wanting to fix them or erase them immediately. One must truly trust the healing process of the deep self to watch emerging patterns and to wait for an unconscious force to heal these.

As the aura is cleared of present life karma, debris presents itself from past lives and lineage issues. During these releases very terrifying things can be presented. People whom I have worked with report such gruesome experiences as being burned in an incinerator by a group of priests, being sacrificed on a stone slab, being chased by an evil shaman and more. During this process people often become spooked to say the least. Certainly at any point in a person's development, he or she may want to seek counseling support or advice from a spiritual teacher. The person can always trust the body sense about when to seek help from whom. In addition, it is essential to stay with a practice of attention. Watch it, feel it—but don't react.

When people get terrified or spooked at this time, they often think that someone is doing something evil to them psychically. And this could be the case. But a person gives this twisted influence more energy by feeding it with fear. It is almost as if a weak spot has been found in the person's aura and the weakness is exaggerated. Therefore, instead of freaking out about an attacking force, it is more effective to clear the mind and hold the attention with the will. This prevents an outside energy from feeding on a person's vulnerability. And it also allows a person to see and release deep-seated inner issues without blaming them on others. Spiritual practice is very important here.

Perhaps a few words are in order about past lives. Shirley MacLaine's work has certainly popularized the notion of working with past lives. Therapists now do past-life regressions. Channelers will tell you what century you lived in, and some will even tell you what planets you came from.

This information could be true, or it could be metaphors and symbols to pay attention to. Or it could be hype. Trust the reaction of the body sense to this information, and remember that a spiritual awakening is a process and not a fact-finding mission. You are not looking for information outside of yourself that will explain your existence. Spending a lot of time on figuring out past lives may prevent you from facing what is inside. You are waking up to the wonders inside yourself which in turn connect you to the universe.

After exposing karmic debris from human lives and human lineage, the next issues that emerge from the unconscious are the archetypes of human existence, deep and ancient. These seem to emerge from the depth of emptiness inside the human aura, out of the base chakra, spiralling up with great energy that cannot be ignored. The entire inner being is filled with this awareness. It is like looking at a piece of velvet at a distance of one inch and having that velvet texture fill the field of vision, but this is inside the mind. Facing these archetypes as they emerge is truly a hero-heroine journey.

The Hero-Heroine, the Shaman and the Evolution of Human Consciousness

One of the major emphases of Joseph Campbell's* work is the documentation of the hero's journey from legends of many different cultures. The commonality in these legends is that a person journeys into the unknown and is tested to the very core of the human experience. Many terrors and demons are faced along the path. The hero-heroine faces the trials and tests with courage and returns with a gift for humanity. The shaman in a similar way makes the same journey. In this age, such a journey plays particular importance in spiritual development.

In the past, great spiritual teachers who had accomplished the integration of spirit into being could actually "do this for" others. By merging into their spirit, they could assist the rest of humanity in taking a small step toward spiritual integration.

Saviors or martyrs through their teachings and/or sacrifices have been able through their acts of purification to help others with their next step in spiritual evolution. Saviors or martyrs are archetypes in the collective unconscious which have aided people in moving towards clarity. Because of the history of these archetypes, people expect someone else to tell them the meaning of their life and to define God. But this strategy no longer works, as can be seen in the crash of many spiritual teachers who begin their career aligned with divine purpose. The fault may not be Rajneesh's or Jimmy Swaggert's. It may be in the fact that other people invested them with psychic power over themselves.

As savior and martyr archetypes are being broken, similarly ancient dominance-submission agreements do not work anymore. These agreements were made so that one person protects while the other person submits. They are no longer useful. Examples of the breaking of these archetypes abound in our current culture. Codependent literature helps people realize that sacrificing oneself for an addict's needs may be a twisted way of meeting esteem needs. Neither the addict, nor the codependent person benefit. Overcoming codependence is a perfect example of the breakup of the martyr archetype, as is the fact that women are rejecting their historic submissive roles. In addition, men are beginning to realize that they, in some way, are victimized by the dominant role of protector and provider.

At this point in time in the evolution of consciousness, humans are learning to balance the four aspects of their being—body, mind, spirit, and emotions. People are integrating the spirit fully into the other dimensions of their being. This allows work with both material and nonmaterial reality. The shift to having more people more fully integrated with their spiritual nature creates a new forum for spiritual work.

Because of this evolution of consciousness, people now need to take the step of total surrender to the spirit within, instead of relying on others to do this for them. At this point a spiritual teacher cannot "save" others, but rather can only create an environment for a fellow human to contact his or her own inner healing force. Nor can a dominant protector keep another person from the dangers of the dark. The inner journey itself, must be taken alone. No one can take that jump into the unknown for another. Others can nurture, push, and energize, but now we are each our own shaman or hero-heroine. In essence, savior or martyr archetypes are being broken.

There is a threshold or a diaphragm-like opening to another world within the self. A person can only enter this place alone in the archetype of a hero, heroine, or shaman. We unite fully with our spirit by journeying into the darkness within and returning with the gift of an integrated being.

Psychic Duels

As people become more clear in their awareness, the aspects of the being are more fully integrated. The spirit is more fused into every aspect. Shamans or light-carriers may notice that others are very attracted to them. People start gravitating toward a full being as if they want to own what that person has.

At these times a person may feel a surge of energy, as in a psychic break. But in this case the energy is coming from outside the person. A psychic duel or challenge could be beginning. One way to frame such an event is that by challenging someone, the other person is strengthening his or her awareness. It is like a person playing a tennis match with someone better to improve his or her skills. This orientation prevents a person from framing the energy surge as an "evil" attack. It is important to sidestep the ego's attempts at thinking that a person is "hot" because someone else wants the focalized light. Psychic duels are very difficult situations. It takes great will to maintain inner clarity. Therefore they are not food for the ego's pride.

A story may be in order to clarify this point. I was working as an administrator of a college. I was told to report to a new person named Sarah. I looked forward to a good, working relationship. However, one day Sarah said she needed to see me. I could tell she was agitated. She said she had heard from a friend who lived in one of my program's sites that the college was doing a terrible job. I tried to explain what we were doing there, but nothing I said seemed to calm her. She became more agitated and started talking about my capabilities to run a program. I had an emotional response of being attacked very deeply in the heart, and then I suggested to Sarah that she should not supervise me so closely.

Afterward I was deeply disturbed for days; my head was spinning and I had a great rending in my heart. I could not really figure out what was happening since it did not seem like a major event. But I had a vision of the scene in Sarah's office. The top of the office split open and Sarah grew very tall and looked down on me. Then I grew taller than Sarah. At that point the side of the office opened up and exposed a deep red-walled canyon that moved back into the wilderness. I picked Sarah up by her feet in the vision and stuffed her upside down into the canyon. After that I felt better. Who knows, this could have been a silly daydream that diffused my anger. But it felt like a major event. I had to stand my ground in all dimensions—physically, emotionally, and psychically—to maintain balance.

Psychic challenges do happen, and usually it is not clear that one has occurred until it is over. Lynn Andrews'* books have great descriptions of psychic duels between medicine men and women, depicting the overpowering nature of such challenges. It is important to note that being challenged does not necessarily mean that one needs to defeat another. Rather, a challenge is an opportunity to shove psychic energy out of one's aura. Imagery is a helpful process to accomplish self-protection in psychic duels. For example, the following imagery could be used:

> Feel your energy go through your feet into the core of the earth. Feel yourself being strongly grounded. Take your attention to a membrane-like perimeter outside your body, about two feet in all directions. See if you can take your attention to all areas of this membrane-like surface. Then take your attention to your heart and with the full force of the will united with the attention, shove the energy you feel impinging in your aura out.

The Friendly Void

In the Buddhist worldview or paradigm, the concept of the void is very important. In this concept all energy stems from and returns to the void. Experientially the void can be seen as a dynamic vortex of undifferentiated energy. The concept of the reversal of the Tao (when moving fully into one polarity, one moves into the opposite polarity) teaches that by merging with the emptiness of the void, a person becomes one with everything.

The void is a great help in facing terrors and demons. The Buddha teaches the exquisite nature of the compassion of the heart when it is in contact with this source of all energy. Possibly the void is the heart of creation. Oddly enough, one can sense this exquisite, oceanic energy of compassion by creating an empty space in the heart. This technique of moving the attention to the heart and opening the heart psychically so that it is empty is very powerful in dealing with challenges and chilling visions.

Death

Joseph Campbell tells us that death is an essential compo-
nent of the hero-heroine journey. The hero or heroine dies to
a certain state of consciousness and is reborn into a totally
different way of knowing or looking at the world. Death is
also central to the shamanic tradition. Most shaman initia-
tions contain what is claimed to be actual death experience
to the physical body, not symbolic death. For example a shaman may experience moving into an opening in the Earth
(i.e., the underworld) and then moving down into a cave with
many crystals in the ceiling. Then the shaman may see a pool
which he enters and the liquid in the pool dissolves his body.
At that point he becomes bones, scattered on the floor of the
cave. The bones then reorganize into a bird. The shaman, now
a bird, screeches and rises through the Earth with great ve-
locity. His speed increases as he exits the Earth and spins out
of the earth's atmosphere. The bird-shaman circles the Earth
and then slowly and gently floats down to Earth. Transforming back to the human form, the shaman walks on the Earth
in a new body, with a new purpose, united with the light.

A person who wants to experience expanded consciousness or chart multiple realities better be ready to face death
after death after death. To become empty one usually dies to
every concept one has on how things should be and what is
important. For example one may be working on dying to the
idea of being something. After being nothing for a time, a
person has to die to nothing and become something. It is
almost as if a person needs to experience each side of the Tao
or each polarity to become one with the formless primordial
energy that is the essence of life or God.

Terrors and demons are great opportunities to die and
to be transformed into a closer and closer incarnation of spirit
fully bonded with matter. Challenges provide each person
with a test, honing the will and intent on surrender towards
the unity with God. Now in this age each of us is prompted

to take the hero-heroine journey and become a shaman light-warrior for the unity of our own being.

Consciousness and the North American Continent

The topography of consciousness on the continent of North America is different than it is for those living in Asia, Europe, or Africa. Consciousness is a result of a complex set of factors, including physical connection to the Earth. Therefore, consciousness may differ at different points on the Earth, depending on the Earth's energy.

The aim of spiritual development is for a person to merge with the spirit self hidden deep in the unconscious. One way to achieve this is to transcend human nature. This approach is found in Christian tradition where the human is born of sin. The human body, desires, and emotions are seen as something to overcome. This is also true in Judaism where rules are used to be aligned with God and to refrain from sin. In addition, some Asian spiritual traditions contain the concept of transcending human nature. Yoga practice teaches that one must overcome the fluctuations of the mind for spiritual union with the God. Similarly, Buddhism specifies that all human suffering is rooted in attachment, and attachment results from human desires, in part.

The North American continent presents different possibilities for spiritual development. The human consciousness, or mind, resonates with the physical environment of habitation. Native North Americans have created an Earth-integrated spiritual tradition. This means that they attempt to identify with nature rather than transcend it. The human experience is embraced in order to *transform* it to the spiritual dimension. It is a matter of imploding through one's humanity into spiritual awareness. The process is one of *transformation* as opposed to *transcendence*, since a transcendent approach seeks to overcome the human experience. Tantric Buddhism also recommends transformation instead of transcendence. According to the Dalai Lama,[1] human senses are not denied, but are used as a part of the spiritual path. Because Tantric Buddhism was strongly influenced by Tibetan shamanism during its inception, and because of the shamanism in North America, Tantric Buddhism may hold some lessons for North Americans. By identifying with nature, North Americans (and the rest of the world!) can learn how they fit in with creation to live in harmony with the primal forces which began this universe. The path toward spirituality is actually merging with "humaness" to align with the spirit that pervades all life.

Our bodies come from the Earth, and hold the connection with nature, which can be a source for spiritual development. A spiritual approach that transcends these human qualities may create struggle, since strong energies must be denied. The North American path, then, is more appropriately an act of bonding with the Earth forces in the body which are visceral, emotional, wild, energetic, and even violent at times. I am not suggesting we act in these ways, but rather that we allow these feelings to emerge within us and sense them fully. In this way we move through them, and become more whole by allowing our most ancient instincts to be heard within our consciousness. People speed their spiritual development by opening to their animal self, where the mysteries of creation lie. The attention is trained to keep with the sometimes violent emotions inside, without acting on them. This creates an accelerated method for exploding the structures within the mind that constrict the spirit. North Americans reap the benefits of the continent's vigorous energy. The Earth's energy is used to merge with our body and emotions on the path to union with the spirit.

---

[4] The Dalai Lama, Tsong-ka-pa, and J. Hopkins. *Tantra in Tibet* (Ithaca, New York: Snow Lion, 1977).

Imagery Exercise: Uniting with the Earth's Core

Sit or lie comfortably. Start relaxing your body and take your attention deep within. Feel the points in which your body contacts the floor. Feel those points growing flatter, so that more of your body is in contact with the floor. Feel your body flattening. Feel the muscles moving away from the bones and the skin moving away from the muscles.

Move your attention throughout your body, starting with your feet, your ankles, your calves, your knees and your thighs. Relax your groin, stomach, heart, and lungs. Open your palms, relax your arms, open your shoulder joints. Feel your whole body slowing down. Relax your neck and head. Release each vertebra. Relax your eyes, your nose, your ears, your mouth, and your tongue. Unlock your jaw, feel your feet growing longer and your head growing taller. Imagine that your face is becoming flatter and rounder.

Now imagine that you are standing outside in a spot that you like. Imagine perceptual details. A sound, a touch, a color, the wind on your cheek, the movement of your limbs. Be in the setting. Become the setting.

Now look down at your feet and notice the color, texture, and density of the Earth under your feet. You feel planted and solid on the Earth. As you look at your feet, you realize that the ground is opening up between your feet. However, you are not scared, you know you will not be physically harmed. As the ground opens you see deeper and deeper into the Earth. Soon not only has the ground opened up but now you are actually moving down through the Earth. You notice the colors and textures as you move down. Deeper and deeper you go down. You know that you can move without hurting yourself. You can still breathe.

Soon you are in the molten core of the Earth. You notice the color, orange-red, and you feel an enormous power in this molten core. You also sense your connection and oneness with it.

After a bit when you are ready, you start moving back up to the surface, slowly and steadily. With you comes this power of the magnetic core that keeps our planet in orbit. You are again standing on the Earth. You have come from the core of the Earth to the surface of the Earth. But you still have the feeling of the strength of the Earth's core. Radiating through your feet into your legs, chest, hands, and head is the Earth's power.

Imagery Story: Vultures and Eagles

This story comes from an imagery group. The group was working on issues of facing the darkness in the unconscious. One woman in the group named Sandra had a meditation practice. She was quite adept at creating a serene, peaceful, stream of consciousness in which she was detached. Earlier in the group work, she had had a strong vision of being an eagle and moving in the circle. She was clawing the Earth in a visceral manner, saying, "This Earth is mine, mine, mine." She felt violent and possessive. She didn't like the vision and wanted to move into the safety of her practiced serene mind. But this vision didn't go away.

At the last group session, the four members in the group created a group vision in which each being was a bird. These birds were interacting in the vision. There was a bird who was half vulture and half eagle, and there were two vultures and one eagle. Sandra was the half vulture and half eagle. She wanted to fly around and attack other birds, but she didn't want to eat other birds. One of the vultures taunted her and said, "Why don't you go to your nest to rest?" The hybrid bird said "I don't want to." The vulture continued, "You have to be half eagle, because you reject the vulture. But I am proud to be a vulture. I am swift, I clean the Earth; I am needed."

At that point Sandra became a full eagle and killed and ate the vulture. The vulture was empowered and strengthened by being taken into the eagle's flesh.

Chapter Seven

Bliss and Peace

My sight was almost like a bird fly-ing. I saw the Earth below me. Maybe it was more like I was an astronaut because I could see the entire form of the North Ameri-can continent. The greenness and the fertileness of the conti-nent was overwhelming. I saw a woman's form appear over the continent and it was if she was growing out of it, centralized in the Great Plains. She had flowing hair and was archetypal but very alive too. I loved her. She was very strong and nurturing. She had a dress that was flowing like her hair. In her hand was a very large hoop. She would make big swinging motions with the hoop in front of her body. With each swing, great abundance would flow out of the hoop. It seemed like a mixture of energy and matter. I was glad that the woman was there and wanted her to con-tinue to swing her hoop.

Life

Many people when they are young have the sensation that they are living in a dream and when they wake up they will know what is really happening. It is a feeling as if there is something else besides what they already know. Sometimes this creates an eerie feeling of uneasiness, as if what is happening is not real. Hinduism contains the concept of maya. One way to interpret maya is that the material world presented to the senses is an illusion or that perception is a reaction of the senses to the spontaneous projection of energy from underlying undifferentiated subtle forces. Maya may explain why some people know that there is something else, more real if you will, than what is coming through their senses. This promotes a natural detachment which is healthy but also may promote a detachment to the experience of life itself. It may appear that in the illusory nature of perceptual sensations that one's life is illusory as well. Of course, this is true on one level, but on another level treating one's life as an illusion prevents the person from fully integrating with the deep self within or with that part that is not an illusion. Each life is sacred and in order to grow spiritually a person needs to bond with the human experience fully. Life is serious in its purpose, although what our conscious mind worries about probably misses the point. Each life is serious and sacred.

Calming the Waves

With much practice a person develops the ability to keep the mind focused on a point, so precise it is like a laser in the third eye. It is an acute psychic awareness. As a person then begins to move through the karmic patterns that unfold from within, this point expands until the whole being is in focus.

Patanjali, a great yoga teacher, wrote the Yoga *Sutras* in the second century B.C. The *Sutras* are 196 terse statements of truth (e.g., successful concentration is direct knowledge). Patanjali equated the chitta (mind stuff) to a body of water with much turbulence and many waves. As the waves are calmed the mind becomes smooth and undisturbed. Some

Westerners who adopt a spiritual practice try to achieve this calm through holding down the waves with the conscious mind. It is as if a pressure is pushed down upon the mind to make the waves flat. But making the waves flat is not the same as calming the waves. Pressuring the mind to create stillness is counterproductive to creating awareness. Instead it is a release of the emotions that in time creates the calm waters. This is accomplished by going through emotions, by sensing them clearly and letting the deep self heal. The paradox of calming the waves by creating more turbulence presents itself.

It is a humbling experience to know that you are supposed to be serene like the Buddha under the bodhi tree, and at the same time have psychic surges explode inside of you. During some of these surges it even takes effort to stay in an upright position. But over time, and this may be years, the chitta unwinds and the deep levels clear out. Then there is a peace. But the peace is not like the conscious mind thinks it will be. It is a dynamic peace of surges and ebbs and human frailty and transcendent bliss. And it is a continual surrender to the universe time and time again.

What is Enlightenment?

When I was a young girl, there was an excellent museum in the city where I lived. It had an outstanding Asian wing with paintings, cricket cases and slabs of marble showing the seasons. There was an ink painting of two Japanese Buddhist monks. They had rags around them and they were laughing. They were beggars who went from town to town. Many people thought they were fools but others knew that they were enlightened.

I loved these two monks. It substantiated my belief that things are really different than most people think they are. You may be walking down the street and walk by an enlightened person. He may be a beggar and you may not recognize him.

The point is that enlightenment is a quality or state of consciousness. It is not a badge or a place of attainment. It is a process. Our conscious mind would love to get control of enlightenment as a commodity. But the people that are enlightened probably wouldn't tell you that they are. They would instead attune their being to the subtle force of God and let the energy of their consciousness speak.

The Child in Each One of Us

Jesus said to come unto God as a little child. People have interpreted this admonishment in many different ways. But possibly innocence and spontaneity are the child's qualities that Jesus was talking about. Little children are naturally intuitive. They know how to sense what is going on and how to feel. We each were once intuitive with a lack of self-consciousness about who we are. That is the state to return to in bringing a developed will and attention to join with God.

An open, child-like heart, a honed awareness, an alive spirit and an empty mind create a dynamic purified being. A poem I wrote at a particularly difficult period of my life helped me maintain a child's heart.

> I am the Buddha's heart.
> I am the Buddha's strength.
> I will fear nothing.
> I will act with insight and clarity.
> I will act in Peace.
> Peace.
> I will be Peace.
> I am Peace.
> I am the Buddha.

The Path Ahead

The impetus for writing this book was experiencing a journey that was shattering, disintegrative, full of states of lethargy and weakness, while at the same time the journey was interspersed with states of bliss, transcendence, and an ever increasing psychic awareness. For those of us in the West on spiritual journeys, there is not much guidance about what to do during shattering emotional states that accompany spiritual growth. If you tell your yoga teacher you are experiencing the "shakes," or psychic energy surges in your body, the teacher is apt to tell you to ignore this and continue your practice. This is sound advice, but it may give you the impression that there is something wrong with what you are experiencing.

Spiritual practitioners need to know that the shakes and other out-of-the-ordinary emotional states are normal experiences as part of spiritual development. They also need to know that there are imagery techniques to help them stay with these states, as the deep self expands the physical, emotional, and mental bodies to accept more and more energy. In addition, it is important that seekers know that humility in the face of healing emotional trauma is essential to their path. Sadness, pain, or emotional fragmentation do not mean that a person is not creating the correct reality. It may mean that healing is occurring.

The spiritual journey will exaggerate people's greatest fears, will expose trauma and will show them that everything they thought they were, they are not. The journey will also magnify the love in the heart for the self and others, will allow one to hear the voices of angels, and will turn one's smile into beneficence.

This book's intent is to complement other spiritual practices and show readers that the spiritual path is one of acceptance, not one of control. The basic approach is accepting whatever occurs on the inside and trusting the spirit self to shift and heal the current state. The process takes patience and endurance, but it works. To be honest, it must be said there is no apparent outcome to be achieved through the many deaths required to release judgment on what is happening inside. The steady state of enlightenment may be that of continual dynamic change. The coyote's howl reminds seekers not to take the human condition too seriously.

Imagery Exercise: Taking Flight

You are outside in a large field, or it could be that you are on the top of a large mesa. In either case, a large flat area extends itself before you. You begin walking. You feel your feet and legs moving. You may notice how it feels for your feet to touch the ground. What are you walking on? Is it sandy? Is it grassy? What do you see around you? Are there trees or bushes? Are there mountains or hills? What colors do you notice? What textures? Could you reach out and touch something, or pick something up? How does it feel in your hand or across your fingers. What does the sky look like? Are there clouds? Is there a wind and do you see trees moving? Look around you. Sense the scene fully. [Pause.]

Now notice that you are walking a bit faster. At the same time, you feel a sensation on top of your shoulder blades. It is an itchy feeling. You are walking faster and faster, almost running now. The feeling on your shoulder blades grows stronger. It is as if something is erupting on your back. [Pause.] You are sprouting wings. Big wings. The wings are starting to move, up and down. You are running and your wings are beating. Soon... yes... soon you take flight. You move off the ground. You feel safe and that your wings can take you where you want to go. You could look at your wings if you like and notice what they are made of, the texture and the color.

Look down as you fly and notice what is below you. [Pause.] Let your image move on its own. Fly to wherever you would like. You can find a perch on a tree or high on a mountain, or you can keep flying. [Pause.] Now come back to the place where you started. You feel your feet on the ground, and your wings shrink away. Come back to this time and place, but don't lose the feeling of flight.

Relationships

This book is about inner experience or the topography of the mind that creates consciousness. But are the book's teachings applicable to outer experiences, particularly those with other people? A premise of the book is that when a person moves fully into the microcosm within, then that person joins the macrocosm of the universe. This macrocosm certainly includes other people.

There is some writing and theories on using relationships as spiritual practice. And truly if one follows the advice in this book, every activity of the day including interacting with other people could serve to integrate the spirit into the being. This is done by surrendering the conscious mind's control and merging the attention fully with the moment of experience. This process can be used to stir a pot, to run, or to take a photograph. Any action or life process can be approached with a mindfulness of watching and *feeling*, but not reacting or figuring out meaning. Relationships, however, seem different. It is difficult to keep the attention focused when a person is interacting with someone else. However, it can be developed, by bringing the attention to the process of interaction and one's body reaction simultaneously. For those people in a relationship, focusing on the process of the relationship will accelerate spiritual development for both parties.

One prerequisite is that both members must approach the relationship with the intention of using the relationship for spiritual growth. In an article in which Ken Wilber* documents his wife's death, he talks of the transformative power of love:

> A phrase from a teacher of ours kept running through my mind: "Practice the wound of love... practice the wound of love." Real love hurts; real love makes you totally vulnerable and open; real love will take you beyond yourself and therefore real love will devastate you.[1]

This quote captures the death and rebirth that is constant in the spiritual path. Relationships can also be used for awakening. Imbuing the process of relationship with meditative attention and fullness of experience can serve to create personal transformation for both members in the relationship. Two consciousnesses combined in their path combine synergistically to accelerate the stripping away of what is not real. Bringing awareness to the process of the relationship means

1) suspending judgment of the experience.

2) paying attention to the internal body sense evoked during an interaction.

3) staying with emotions that arise during the interaction.

4) expressing these emotions without judging the other person, or judging oneself for having the emotion.

In short, the emphasis is on the *experience* of the relationship and allowing the deep self to guide the unfolding. In other words, a person applies the teachings of *Living the Wheel* to the dynamic interaction between two people.

An example of a couple's interaction may clarify how this works. Shakti Dawn and Shiva Sunset have been seeing

---

[2] Wilber, K. 1989. "For a Star Dakini." *Common Boundary*. May/June, p. 10.

each other for two years and living together for four months. Shakti doesn't like the way Shiva has taken over cleaning the house. It feels to her that he is implicitly judging her lifestyle. At the same time she really appreciates his help and feels that she is being defensive. Shiva, on the other hand, doesn't understand why Shakti can't see that keeping the house in order on a regular basis will make cleaning easier.

Shakti says, overcoming her internal struggle about whether her emotions are valid (remember, all emotions are valid), "I feel judged by your cleaning up the house all the time. It seems like you think it is a mess."

"I'm not judging, I'm helping," responds Shiva.

"It doesn't feel like help. It feels like you are upset by the way things are."

"I don't mean to judge. This is just my way of helping. I feel attacked by you now."

This type of exchange may go on for several hours or days. The important thing is that each person is staying with her or his emotions and expressing them. Both have to trust that the deep healing force inside of each will provide a shift in the pattern, so that the interaction becomes "unstuck." Sometimes this process feels as if one is wading in mud. However, in time perspectives change and understanding comes.

The key is not to opt out and say, "This isn't working. You never listen. You're always right and I'm wrong," or to seek control through guilt or intimidation, "You never listen. You are just being selfish." It takes trust in one's own inner self and the inner self of one's companion.

This process should sound familiar because it is the same one applied to one's inner experience. You experience, watch, and wait for the inner process to shift things. The difference here is that a person is talking about what is going on inside to another person as it occurs. This interactive process can be as difficult. You die to what you think should be happening and the judgments you have of the other person and yourself. There are times of aloneness when one needs to go in-

side and nurture and heal oneself. There are times of difficulty in the interactions. But there is always the feeling of
movement and cleansing.

Bringing awareness to the relationship process is fulfill-
ing and highly rewarding. The journey of two growing into
integrated beings is profound in its effects. Another quote
from Wilber in the same article summarizes the process:

> We simply and directly served each other, exchang-
> ing self for other, and therefore glimpsing that eter-
> nal spirit. Spirit which transcends both self and
> other.[2]

---

[2] Wilber, K. 1989. "For a Star Dakini." *Common Boundary*. May/June, p.11.

Who's Who

Lynn Andrews
A woman from Beverly Hills who studied with an Indian medicine woman. Some have called her a female Carlos Castenada. There is controversy on the authenticity. However, her books contain some of the most vivid accounts of the terrors of dealing in multiple realities. They convey the *experience* of altered state work.

Medicine Woman. New York: HarperCollins, 1981

Jeanne Achterberg
A practicing pyschologist whose work is on the relationship of imagery with the body's physiological functioning. She has shown that she can increase levels of specific cells, like killer T-cells, which attack cancer cells. She does this by showing patients physiologically accurate photos of cells and having them image increases of these cells in the body.

Imagery in Healing: Shamanism and Modern Medicine. Boston: Shambhala, 1985.

David Bohm
An American physicist who integrates a Hindu view of reality with his research in particle physics. His spiritual perspective is most closely aligned with Krishnamurti.

Wholeness and the Implicate Order. London & Boston: Routledge and Kegan Paul,1980.

Joseph Campbell

A scholar of mythology who spent many years identifying the core teachings across many of the world's myths and religions. He taught us that the unconscious is accessed through metaphors in stories and myths.

The Hero with a Thousand Faces. Princeton, NJ: Princeton University Press, 1972.

Ram Dass

Formerly Richard Alpert, a child psychologist at Harvard, who experimented with LSD along with Timothy Leary. Ram Dass traveled to India and studied with a guru. He is a leading force in the integration of Western pyschology with Eastern practices to awaken spiritual development.

Be Here Now. Boulder, CO: Hanuman Foundation, 1971.

The Only Dance There Is. New York: J. Aranson, 1976.

Mircea Eliade

A Romanian who did the seminal documentation of shamanic work.

Shamanism: Archaic Techniques of Ecstasy. Princeton, NJ: Princeton University Press, 1972.

Sigmund Freud

The father of Western psychology who was the first to articulate clearly the existence of the unconscious mind. He believed that we were motivated primarily by sexual drive. His work is dated, but the basic idea of the unconscious and how the energy of the mind works is helpful.

An Outline of Psycho-Analysis. New York: W. W. Norton & Company, 1949.

Baba Hari Das
An East Indian who has established a yoga center, Mount Madona. He teaches raja or royal yoga which consists of eight limbs or branches moving from moral teachings to samadhi or oneness with the Godhead.

Silence Speaks: From the Chalkboard of Baba Hari Das. Santa Cruz, CA. Sri Rama Foundation, 1977.

Joan Halifax
An anthropologist who documented visions of shamans.

Shamanic Voices: A Survey of Visionary Narratives. New York: HarperCollins, 1979.

Jean Houston
A current psychologist who integrates theology, psychology, and altered states of consciousness. She uses imagery, a sense of what she calls the kinesthetic body, and Greek mythology to merge individuals' experience with their deep purpose.

The Search for the Beloved: Journeys in Sacred Psychology. Los Angeles: Jeremy P. Tarcher, 1987.

Carl Jung
One of Sigmund Freud's students who shifted Freud's focus from sexual motivation into his own brand of psychoanalysis. His main contribution was the proposal of the collective unconscious or a primal dimension shared by all humans where archetypes which motivate our behavior reside. Current followers of Jung give the name *depth psychology* to their work.

Analytical Psychology. New York: Moffat, Yard, 1916. Available today as *Analytical Psychology: Its Theory and Practice.* New York: Random House, 1970.

The Archetypes and the Collective Unconscious, Princeton, NJ: Princeton University Press, 1968. This can be found in volume 9, I, of the Bolligen Series XX of *The Collected Works of C. G. Jung,* trans. R.F.C. Hull. Princeton, NJ: Princeton University Press, 1959, 1969.

Carl Lashley

A famous neuroscientist who worked in the early 20th century to discover the site of memory in the brain mass. He, like most brain researchers, ended up in awe over the brain. Researchers find that the more you know about the brain, the more questions you have.

Brain Mechanisms and Intelligence: A Quantitative Study of Injury to the Brain. Chicago: University of Chicago Press, 1929.

Abraham Maslow

The founding force of humanistic psychology who studied individuals who were noted for "peak experiences" or transcendent states of unity. Based on this study, he postulated that each of us had an actualizing tendency that would lead us through need levels going from survival to self-transcendence.

Motivation and Personality. New York: HarperCollins, 1970.

Takeshi Masui

A Japanese clinical psychologist whose work integrates creating metaphors of emotions in the body through images. He then has individuals shift the metaphors by shifting the image, without figuring out meaning.

The Patient's Efforts and Psychotherapy: The Images of Symptoms. Presented at the 3rd International Imagery Conference, Fukuoka, Japan, 1987.

Frederick Perls
A psychologist associated with the humanistic psychology movement. He was strongly influenced by Eastern spiritual philosophy and concentrated on developing awareness in the moment and a body sense of emotions.

Gestalt Therapy Verbatim. ed. by John Stevens. Lafayette, CA: Real People Press, 1969.

Karl Pribram
A neuroscientist at Stanford who did research with Lashley and later did his own research. He now proposes a holographic model of the mind, in which each piece stores an imprint of the whole and in which thinking is not in synapse firing, but in slow wave fronts across the brain.

Languages of the Brain: Experimental Paradoxes and Principles in Neuropsychology. New York: Brandon House, 1981.

Swami Rama
A teacher of yoga philosophy and holistic health who founded the Himalayan International Institute of Yoga Science and Philosophy in Honesdale, Pennsylvania. He does an outstanding job of integrating yoga philosophy with Western psychology.

Swami Rama, Ballentine, R., and Ajaya, S., *Yoga and Psychotherapy: The Evolution of Consciousness.* Honesdale, PA: Himalayan International Institute, 1976.

Carl Rogers
Another central figure in humanistic psychology. He created techniques to adapt the concept that each person has an innate healing force in the unconscious to counseling settings. He created conditions to use in a therapeutic setting which would allow this force to unfold.

On Becoming a Person: A Therapist's View of Psychotherapy. Boston: Houghton Mifflin, 1961.

Freedom to Learn. New York: C. E. Merrill, 1969.

Ken Wilber

One of the major spokesmen in the field of transpersonal psychology, a field which incorporates the spiritual dimension into the study of the human condition. He integrates many ancient Eastern traditions in explaining the evolution of human consciousness. He proposes a strong intellectual analysis and a hiearchical view of conscious experience. He is also a strong advocate of adopting a spiritual practice from an ancient tradition.

Up from Eden: A Transpersonal View of Human Evolution. Garden City, NY: Anchor Press/ Doubleday, 1981.

The Holographic Paradigm and Other Paradoxes. Boston: Shambhala, 1987.

Imagery Readings

Imagery and Sports Performance

Nideffer, R. M. *Athlete's Guide to Mental Training*. Champaign, IL: Human Kinetics Publishers, 1985.

Imagery and Cognitive Psychology

Hebb, D. O. (1968). "Concerning Imagery." *Psychological Review* 75: 466-477.

Pinker, S. and Kosslyn, S. M. "Theories of Mental Imagery." In A. A. Sheikh, *Imagery: Current Theory, Research and Applications*. New York: John Wiley & Sons, 1983, 43-71.

Imagery and Learning

Levin, Joel R. "Educational Applications of Mnemonic Pictures: Possibilities Beyond Your Wildest Imagination." In A. A. Sheikh and K. S. Sheikh. *Imagery in Education: Imagery in Education Processes*. Farmingdale, NY: Baywood Publishing Company, 1985, 63-87.

Murdock, M. *Spinning Inward: Using Guided Imagery for Children for Learning, Creativity and Relaxation*. Boston and London: Shambhala, 1987.

Ryan, E. B., Ledger, G. W. and Weed, K. A. (1987). "Acquisition and Transfer of an Integrative Imagery Strategy by Young Children." *Child Development* 58: 443-452.

Speidel, G. E. and Troy, M. E. "The Ebb and Flow of Mental Imagery in Education." In A. A. Sheikh and K. S. Sheikh, *Imagery in Education: Imagery in Education Processes.* Farming-dale, NY: Baywood Publishing, 1985, 11-38.

Imagery, Psychoneuroimmunology and Psychoneurology

Achterberg, J. *Imagery in Healing: Shamanism and Modern Medicine.* Boston: Shambhala, 1985.

Farah, M. J. (1984). "The Neurological Basis of Mental Imagery: A Componential Analysis." *Cognition* 18: 245-272.

Fromme, D. K. and Daniel, J. (1984). "Neurolinguistic Programming Examined: Imagery, Sensory Mode, and Communication." *Journal of Counseling Psychology* 31: 387-390.

Goldstein, L. (1984). "A Reconsideration of Right Hemispheric Activity During Visual Imagery, REM Sleep, and Depression." *Research Communications in Psychology, Psychiatry and Behavior* 9: 139-148.

Hall, S. S. (1989). "A Molecular Code Links Emotions, Mind and Health." *Smithsonian* (June), 62-71.

Nelson, A. (1987). "Imagery's Physiological Base: The Limbic System, a Review Paper. *Journal of the Society for Accelerative Learning and Teaching* 13: 363-373.

Norris, P. "Clinical Psychoneuroimmunology: Strategies for Self-Regulation of Immune System Responding." In J. Basmahian, ed. *Biofeedback Principles and Practice for Clinicians.* Baltimore: Williams & Wilkins, 1989, 57-66.

Rider, M. S., Floyd, J. W., Kirkpatrick, J. (1985). "The Effect of Music, Imagery and Relaxation on Adrenal Corticosteroids and the Re-entrainment of Circadian Rhythms." *Journal of Music Therapy* 12: 46-58.

Rossman, M. *Healing Yourself: A Step-by-Step Program for Better Health Through Imagery.* New York: Pocket Books, 1987.

Springer, S. P. and Deutsch, G. *Left Brain, Right Brain.* San Francisco: W.H. Freeman and Co., 1981.

Imagery and Creativity - Writing, Problem Solving

Brown, G. W. and Wolf, J. S. (1986). "Development of Intuition in the Gifted." *Journal for the Education of the Gifted* 9: 157-164.

Nelson, A. *How to Focus the Distractible Child.* Saratoga, CA: R & E Publishers, 1984.

Rose, R. "Guided Fantasies in Elementary Classrooms." In J. E. Shorr, G. E. Sobel, P. Robin and J. A. Connella, *Imagery: Its Many Dimensions and Applications.* New York: Plenum Press, 1979, 281-289.

VanKrevelen, A. (1983). "Evoking Creative Imagery in Children Using Guided Fantasy." *Academic Psychology Bulletin* 5: 85-89.

Imagery and Spirit: Altered States

Giesler, P. V. (1984). "Batcheldorian Psychodynamics in the Umbanda Ritual Trance Consultation." *Parapsychology Review* (November/December), 5-9.

Harner, M. *The Way of the Shaman.* New York: Bantam Books, 1982.

Houston, J. *The Search for the Beloved: Journeys in Sacred Psychology.* Los Angeles: Jeremy P. Tarcher, 1987.

West, M. A. *The Psychology of Meditation.* Atlanta GA: Clarendon Press, 1987.

Imagery and Emotions - Stress Reduction, Healing Trauma

Ahsen, A. (1982). "Imagery in Perceptual Learning and Clinical Application." *Journal of Mental Imagery* 6: 157-186.

Cerney, M. S. "'If Only . . .' Remorse in Grief Therapy." In *Psychotherapy and the Remorseful Patient*. Binghamton, NY: Haworth Press, 1989.

Gallegos, E. S. (1983). "Animal Imagery, the Chakra System and Psychotherapy." *Journal of Transpersonal Psychology* 15 (2), 125-136.

Jordan, C. S. (1984). "Psychophysiology of Structural Imagery in Post-Traumatic Stress Disorder." *Journal of Mental Imagery* 8: 51-66.

Imagery and Brain Physiology

What is the physiology of thought? Most people concentrate on neuron firing when they study the brain. They assume that thought occurs at the site where a group of neurons fire. Neurons are cells that are unique to the human nervous system (see figure 11, p. 142). A neuron has a specific end called an axon. Neurotransmitters or chemicals within the brain move to the end of an axon and then create an electrical charge that jumps from one axon to the axon of another cell, similar to the action of a spark plug. The space between the two axons is called the synapse. This electrical action across a synapse is called firing.

Karl Pribram[1] speculates that thought does not happen at a specific site in the brain as a group of neurons fire, but rather he proposes that thought occurs as wave patterns move across the brain. Neurons also have other ends that are called dendrites, which usually do not have connections to other cells. Neurons have one axon, but can have many dendrites. Pribram says that once a neuron fires or jumps across the space between two axons, energy in the form of waves also passes from dendrite to dendrite across cells. This then creates slow wave patterns across the network of dendrites throughout the brain. In other words, we don't think as a result of a specific set of neurons firing; but we think as waves move across the brain. This may explain why scientists have

---

[1] Pribram, K.H. *Language of the Brain: Experimental Paradoxes and Principles in Neuropsychology.* New York: Brandon House, 1981.

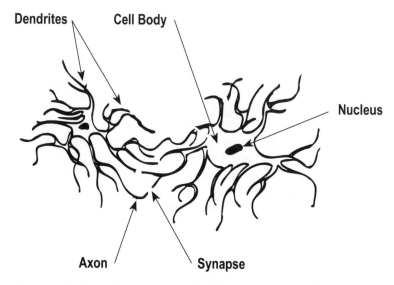

Figure 11. The physiology of neurons.

difficulty in locating thought and why the brain may act as a hologram in its functioning.

Pribram worked for a very famous neuroscientist named Carl Lashley[2]. Lashley was looking for the location of the "engram" or the site of a memory within the brain mass. Lashley taught rats mazes and then cut out part of their brains to see if the memory of the maze was stored in that part. He could cut out 80% of the rats' memory, and they still could perform the maze. Lashley decided that there was no memory. But Pribram postulated that memory may be stored throughout the brain mass instead of at a specific location. Pribram has proposed a holographic model of brain functioning in which each piece of the brain contains the imprint of the entire brain. Thinking then, is a result of wave patterns across the brain, as opposed to action in a

---

[2] Lashley, C.K. *Brain Mechanisms and Intelligence: A Quantitative Study of Injury to the Brain.* (Chicago: University of Chicago Press, 1929).

given spot of the brain. Support for this is that large portions of the brain can be damaged and memory can stay intact. Remaining brain mass, also, will spontaneously take over functions formerly performed by damaged sections of the brain. According to Pribram, the larger the brain mass involved in thought, the more in focus the hologram will become.

Other brain researchers propose alternatives to the simplistic notion that thought is neuron firing. An article in *Science News*[3] shows that many of the same neurons (brain cells) are fired for many different thoughts.

The researchers in this article thought that 5 to 20,000 neurons would be fired in a cat's brain while the cat was learning to choose a door with special markings to find food. However, to their great surprise they found that 5-100,000 million cells were fired during the learning task, or one-tenth of the brain mass. If only specific cells were used in specific memories then the brain mass would be used up after learning only a few things. Obviously the thinking process is more complex than thousands of neurons firing for each thought.

Another neuroscientist, W. Ross Adey[4], proposes that thinking occurs at the surface of the cell when electromagnetic packets of proteins are released. This makes the cell surfaces vibrate and "whisper" to other cells as the vibration is transferred.

Pribram, Adey, and others teach us that thought is a holistic process, using vibrations over the entire brain mass, instead of a firing in one location. This has implications for working with the mind to create altered states and experience multiple realities. A thought process, such as imagery, that is holistic in nature would have the best chance of accessing the most material in the unconscious.

---

[3]Bower, B. 1986. "Million Cell Memories." *Science News* 130: 313-315.
[4]Adey, W. Ross in "Million Cell Memories." *Science News* 130: 313-315.

The Limbic System and Imagery

Research on human thought usually concentrates on the human cortex and its functions, since this is the part of the brain that involves higher order thinking skills (see figure 12).

In some of Karl Pribram's work, he experimented with how stimulation of various parts of the brain affected the field of perception. He found that the field of perception was narrowed when the cortex was stimulated with electrical current. This means that the field of vision would become very focused. For example, if one were looking at a pencil, one would see the details of the pencil such as the color of band around the top of the pencil or the eraser.

Pribram also stimulated the limbic system to find out what would happen. The limbic system is an ancient part of the brain that all mammals have, often termed the paleo–mammalian brain. Since it is seen as a more primitive part of the brain, it is often considered unimportant in human cognition. The limbic system regulates emotion, motivation, attention, and memory, and it is involved with autonomic nervous system activity such as breathing and blood pressure. The limbic system lies underneath the cortex. Pribram discovered

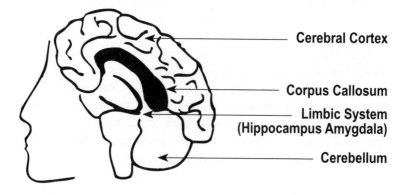

Figure 12. Cross-section of the brain.

that when the limbic system was stimulated, then the field of perception was expanded. One would now see the pencil, plus a lot of things surrounding the pencil—the desk, the floor, and the window. Pribram locates intuition in the limbic system and states that this part of the brain receives temperature sensations from the senses. These perceptions are not localized in time and space. This means that this part of the brain may be involved in expanded states of consciousness that are outside of a time and space dimension.

The limbic system is responsible for intuition and also may mediate expanded perception and sensations without a time or space dimension, such as states of unity with all life or feelings of oceanic bliss. In addition, this part of the brain contains high concentrations of endorphins, the brain's natural opiate, which create states like "runner's high." By learning to use the intuition, the brain's functions of expanded perception and states of well being and bliss are accessed.

Imagery and the Right Brain/Left Brain Notion

The right brain/left brain model of human cognition is used in many sources about working with altered states of reality. The cerebral cortex of the brain has two hemispheres that look identical but appear to have different functions. The hemispheres are joined by a bundle of 200 million nerve fibers called the corpus callosum.

In the 1940s a surgeon named William Van Wagenen[5] had an idea for controlling epileptic seizures. Since an epileptic seizure is an uncontrolled firing of neurons across the brain, Van Wagenen's theory was that by severing the corpus callosum, the seizure would be contained in one hemisphere.

---

[5]Springer, S. P. and Deutsch, G. *Left Brain, Right Brain* (San Francisco, CA: W. H. Freeman and Company, 1981).

The split-brain surgery, a commissurotomy, was performed on about twenty people. At first it seemed that the people were very much the same. However, later the people would be found to be doing very weird things, like putting on a sock with the left hand and trying to take it off with the right. Further research showed that after cutting the corpus callosum, information could not pass from one hemisphere to another. The hemispheres could not talk to each other, so that information received by one hemisphere could not be expressed by another.

It appeared that the hemispheres had very different functions. For example, one split-brain subject when asked to pick out a spoon, could say the word *spoon* but could not find the spoon under a blanket [through the sense of touch]. Linguistic functions appeared to be on one side, the left, and visual-spatial functions appeared to be on the other side, the right.

This led to the right brain/left brain model which localized functions in each of the hemispheres. In this model the left brain is linear, analytical, and linguistic. The right brain is holistic, visual, and imagistic. The left brain processes information successively, one thing after another, and the right brain processes information simultaneously taking in information all at one time.

Utility of the Right Brain/Left Brain Model

This model is helpful in making it clear that there is more than one basic cognitive process in the mind. Before this model, the right hemisphere was called the inferior one, and language was seen as the primary means of thinking. However, the right brain/left brain model makes it clear that the two basic processes of the brain are equally important. Both the linguistic and imagistic functions are critical to human cognition. Linguistic thought is essential for communication, generalization and conceptual development. Imagistic thought is equally as important for creativity, memory, and mind-body communication.

However, there are some shortcomings to the model. First individuals vary as to what functions are in which hemisphere. Sally Springer and George Deutsch, neuroscientists at the State University of New York at Stony Brook, report differences among men and women on cerebral hemisphere functions. Men appear to have visual spatial clearly in the right hemisphere and language in the left. This creates such capabilities as creating visual spatial maps and rotating them. It may also indicate a difficulty in integrating emotions into experiences, since functions are clearly divided and not integrated. There is some evidence that the right hemisphere in males may be somewhat larger, since it is affected by the male hormone testosterone as the male fetus develops.

Women, on the other hand, usually have language distributed across both hemispheres, which may help them integrate language with experiences easily. It also may explain women's so-called "intuition." Distribution of functions across hemispheres may create an ability to take in the whole perceptual scene and pick up peripheral information.

Martha Farah[6] in an article in *Cognition* in 1984 examined patients with brain damage who reported that they could no longer dream, a form of imagery. Dreaming is supposedly a right brain function. These patients had lesions in the posterior region of the *left* hemisphere. The right brain/left brain model may not always work.

It seems clear that the brain is much more complex than a simple right brain/left brain model would suppose. This model has been useful in expanding what our culture de-

---

[6]Farah, M. J. 1984. "The Neurological Bases of Mental Imagery: A Componential Analysis." *Cognition* 2: 55-76.

fines as thinking. But it is essentially incorrect, since the corpus callosum is sending information back and forth between the hemispheres at all times. In addition, the model is dichotomous in nature and promotes people assuming that one kind of thinking is better than the other. New agers can be heard saying that they used to be left brain but now they are becoming right brain.

Imagery may not be right brain, or it may occur in the right brain in some people and in the left brain of others. As Karl Pribram proposes, it may be mediated by the limbic system, a structure below and threaded through the two cortical hemispheres. Regardless of its location, thinking imagistically is integral to a variety of cognitive functions in the mind, body, emotions, and spirit.

Imagery and Psychoneuroimmunology

One of the most exciting areas of study in psychology today is psychoneuroimmunology, or the relationship of the biochemistry of thought and how this affects the immune system.

Up until the last several years, scientists have assumed that the nervous system and the lymphatic or immune system were separate. But Candace Pert and Michael Ruff of the National Institute of Health have documented the amazing interconnection of the two systems.[7] Pert was the first to report the existence of endorphins. Endorphins are a type of neuropeptides which are chemical messengers that create firing or inhibition at the gap (synapse) between two cells. Scientists had noticed that opiates such as heroin already had

---

[7] There are two interesting articles that mention their work. See Weschler, B. (1987). "A New Prescription: Mind Over Malady." *Discovery* (February) 51-61; and Hall, S.S. (1989). "A Molecular Code Links Emotions, Mind and Health." *Smithsonian* (June) 62-71.

receptor sites in neural cells, implying the existence of a natural opiate in the body. Pert demonstrated that one existed in the form of endorphins. Rhythmic stimulation as in running or meditation or breathing exercises of yoga seem to stimulate endorphin release and create a natural high. Oddly enough there are large concentrations of endorphin receptor sites around the limbic system, that part of the brain mediating imagery. This may explain imagery's role in activating relaxed and blissful states.

There are at least fifty neuropeptides, and they are interchangeable. A neuropeptide is made of a string of amino acids which can recombine and reform to make each one of these neuropeptides. These strings of amino acids become a three dimensional key that is the exact shape needed to fit into a neural receptor site.

Pert says that there are "hot spots" for neuropeptide formation and for the location of neuropeptide receptors. These hot spots are in the frontal cortex and in the amygdala and the hippocampus of the limbic system. Since these areas of the brain are closely tied with processing incoming perceptions and in generating emotions, emotions are closely tied with immune activity.

A practical example of the relationship of emotions to healing is the case of Norman Cousins[8] who cured himself of cancer by renting Laurel and Hardy movies and laughing and laughing. Pert claims that a neuropeptide can latch onto a cell generated by the immune or lymphatic system and change its speed and direction. Emotions affect immune response, explaining the inter-connectedness of the nervous system with the immune system and Cousins' success with healing himself with laughter. Both neurons and immune cells have receptors for neuropeptides; the same key activates both systems. Emotions are linked to neuropeptide activity and neuropeptides can affect immune functioning.

---

[8] Cousins. N. *Anatomy of an Illness as Perceived by the Patient: Reflections on Healing and Regeneration* (New York: Norton, 1979).

In a June 1989, *Smithsonian* issue, Pert is quoted as having a recurrent dream in which she is standing on one side of a chasm and a voice is telling her to jump. One side of the chasm is the old medicine and the other side is the new medicine. The new medicine may contain answers on how to use the biochemistry of mental phenomena to affect health through immune activity.

The physiology of imagery makes it a likely candidate for affecting emotions which in turn can affect neuropeptide activity and influence immune response. Two of the three hot spots for neuropeptide activity are the two structures of the limbic system—the amygdala and the hippocampus. Imagery is mediated by the limbic system and is emotionally laden since the amygdala is responsible for emotional memories. Because of this, it seems possible that imagery can directly affect immune response. In fact, Jeanne Achterberg[9] has demonstrated that when people visualized increases in an immune cell, then the number of those cells in blood samples increased. Imagery seems central in evoking effective immune response and in maintaining physical health.

Summary

The process of thought is holistic and defies a linear explanation. It may be explained by synapse firing or slow wave patterns moving across dendrites or "whisper" vibrations emanating from neural cell membranes. The point is that science has not defined the actual physiological process of thought, but it does appear that thought involves large sections of brain mass and not an event in a single location.

Even though most researchers focus on the cortex in studying the human brain, the limbic system appears to play a significant role in emotions, motivation, attention, memory,

---

[9]Achterberg, J. *Imagery in Healing: Shamanism and Modern Medicine* (Boston: New Science Library, Shambhala, 1985).

and immune activity. Since imagery is mediated at the site of the limbic system it implies that the thought process of imagery can affect these functions in human cognition. There is biochemical evidence that imagery is the primitive language of the body, verified by the fact that imagery can increase given cell levels. This supports the use of imagery as: a conduit into the unconscious mind, an effective tool in creating healing physiology in the body, the vehicle to altered states of consciousness, and a ticket to travel in multiple realities. Imagery opens the doors of perception to the worlds in the unconscious.

Imagery Scripts

This appendix is designed to help readers use imagery with individuals or groups. Presented here are general guidelines using components that work well in a sample imagery session. They include the following:

1) *Predetermined Goal or Symbol:* This goal (or symbol) can be determined by the leader based on his or her intuition about what is needed. People usually need practice in imagery before deep issues can be dealt with during the sessions. Sometimes the goal of the imagery can just be practicing to use all senses or becoming familiar with one's unique style of imagery. People often have expectations of how they are to image. Some people have images that flit back and forth or change rapidly; others don't see things but hear music, while others see vague forms. It is important to assure participants in an imagery session that any method is fine. Some people are resistant to doing any imagery at all; these people are usually very uncomfortable in being out of control of what is happening in their minds. They also may be resistant to opening any issue in the unconscious. The best strategy for working with these people is to tell them that they do not need to image. Instead of imaging, they can use the time to relax. Over time, they may begin imaging and profit from the experience. It is important that participants embrace and accept their individual style of imaging and stay with it until it changes of its own accord.

A good initial goal is to help participants create symbols of inner strength, as in power animal imagery. This can give confidence in the process, and the feeling that there are inner resources available to guide and heal. After working with a group or a person, a leader's intuition may give him or her an image to use as the central goal of the next imagery session. For example, I was working with one group who verbalized that they wanted to move into the unconscious, but I felt a lot of resistance to surrendering conscious control of the imagery process. It seemed to me that group members had a lot of unexpressed fears about this surrender. I wanted to make it safe for them to enter the unconscious mind. I had the idea of using a cave, deep in a dark, moist, wood as a metaphor for the unconscious. I added protection by having them start the scene in a bedroom that they had once lived in and where they were happy. I also added each person's child self. Before they left the bedroom, I asked them to put on capes and a hat, and to take up a sword or shield for both their adult and child self. The mythic journey script, which is Imagery Script 4 (on p. 165), came from these ideas. As in the mythic journey script, a leader can use his or her intuition to come up with an imagery exercise. I think it works best if the leader has one or two central images to build the exercise around. In the description above the two central images were the cave and the "safe" bedroom.

2) *Relaxation Instructions:* It is important that the imagery leader begin a session by taking the time to relax the participant(s). Being truly relaxed is a gift that does not happen too often in our culture; therefore, it is a true service to the people you are working with to really take time to help them relax.

Sometimes people will go to sleep during imagery. I think this is okay. Transcendental meditation instructors used to say that if you go to sleep when you meditate, then you must need to sleep. The whole purpose of imagery training is to get people to stop trying with their conscious mind and bond with their inner process through acceptance. Accepting the fact that one goes to sleep during imagery or that one needs rest may be important.

3) *All Senses:* It helps to use all senses during an imagery exercise to achieve the goal of having participants bond with the imagery that they are creating. After relaxation, a helpful technique is to start with a scene and have the participants use all senses in the scene. This is done by asking participants to notice perceptual details (e.g., What color is the table? What would the table feel like if you touched it?).

4) *Establish Trust:* Make everything okay with imagery (i.e., eyes open, eyes closed, follow instructions or not). The only critical variable is for people to take comfortable positions so they will not need to move during the imagery exercise.

5) *Schedule Imagery Regularly:* Imagery ability improves with practice. Also issues that emerge during imagery often need to be looked at many times for release or resolution.

6) *Talk Slowly and Leave Long Pauses.*

7) *Vivify Imagery:* By beginning with drumming or by using music during instructions, create an animated and vivid imagery session.

8) *Encourage Image Movement:* When images move or change on their own accord, the underlying matrix of the unconscious mind is active. This means that a person's deep self is directing the imagery.

9 *Use Transitions:* Pay attention to transitions in images. It is important that you don't change scenes too fast or in a confusing way, so the conscious mind is not activated to figure out what is happening. "How did we get to this planet?" or "How can I breathe under water?" Keep instructions simple and make sure a careful transition is built in when scenes change.

10) *Trust Your Intuition:* You can usually feel if an imagery exercise is working or not. Make sure you stay with your intuition so that it can guide you as you lead the imagery. If you feel a positive shift in the energy of the room, participants really like it when you praise the effort.

11) *Close-up Imagery:* Closing up an imagery exercise is essential. The unconscious has been opened and the deep self has been allowed to speak. Most people are not comfortable with this process if it occurs in their normal waking reality. Therefore it is helpful to close up the unconscious until the participant is ready to work again. This is done by creating a scene of safety or security at the end of the session.

12) *Debrief:* There are many ways to debrief sessions. These include asking people to share what happened, having participants write down their experiences, asking participants to tell a partner what happened, or having people draw something from the imagery. Discourage people from trying to figure out what happened. Instead ask them to describe in detail what they saw and what happened in the imagery. The idea is for the person to wait for insight on the meaning of the imagery.

Do not judge a person's image, even if it is negative or violent. If an individual is in discomfort with an image, the leader can lead the person to some resolution or distance from the image.

Imagery Scripts

The following section contains several scripts. The two initial scripts are samples of relaxation and closing-up instructions that a leader can use at the beginning and end of any imagery exercise. Even though scripts are detailed here, it is important to note that these are just guidelines and ideas. After practicing with these scripts, your intuition is the best source for imagery instructions. Always remember to keep it simple, give the participant time to image and use all senses. The end of each of the chapters also contains imagery script suggestions. These scripts are:

Aligning to the Earth (page 17);

Body Relaxation (page 31). Content overlaps *Transforming Pain*;

Transforming Pain (page 33);

The Child (page 53). Content overlaps *Imagery Script 3* on page 165;

Transforming Emotions (page 81). This is a very important imagery exercise to learn. If you can teach your clients or students to do this one, they can be empowered to continue to release karma and suppressed material from the unconscious;

Power Animal (page 98). Content overlaps *Imagery Script 1* on page 161;

Uniting with the Earth's Core (page 117).

Relaxation Script

This can be used at the beginning of any imagery exercise. I am indebted to my yoga training in the B.K.S. Iyengar tradition for the strategy of using the physiological structure of the body to create deep relaxation.

Either have the participants lie down or sit with their backs supported. Also ask them to uncross legs and arms. Tell them they can close their eyes or not close them; they can follow the imagery directions or not. Also if their imagery starts taking on a life of its own, tell them that they should go with that instead of trying to stay with the instructions. It is fine to use the time to relax. Once participants seem ready, begin leading them through the following relaxation script.

Move your body around for a while until you feel comfortable. You can wiggle a little until you find a comfortable position. As you settle in, feel your body become warmer and heavier. Give yourself permission to slow down.

Take your attention to the very tips of your toes. You feel a little sensation at the end of your right big toe. It is almost as if a cell at the tip of your toe has been charged. You may want to see a butterfly land on the tip of the toe. When the butterfly lands on the toe, there is a slight charge in that spot. Now take your attention to the next toe on your right foot, your middle toe, the fourth toe, and your little toe. Each time the butterfly lands, there is a little sensation or spark at the end of the toe. If you can bring your attention to the very tip of your extremities, you will activate the life force to flow through your entire body.

Now move your attention to your left big toe. There is a little charge. You move to the second toe, the middle toe, the fourth toe, and the little toe on your left foot. There is a charge each time.

You start to feel the energy of your body flow out of your feet. Imagine that the soles of your feet have been peeled away and energy is pouring out of both of your feet.

Relax your right ankle, your right calf, and your right kneecap. Take your attention under the kneecap and release it. Relax your left thigh and go deep in the muscle layers of this muscle. Open your right hip joint. Visualize the ball and socket of this joint and psychically move the ball out slightly, by moving the image.

Relax your left ankle, your left calf, and your left kneecap. Relax your left thigh and move into the layers of that muscle with your attention. Open your left hip joint, see the ball of the joint move out slightly as you did on your right side. As you open your left hip joint feel the energy pour out of that joint into your leg, through your knee, and then out your foot. Feel the same sensation on your right side.

Relax your stomach, your intestines, your pancreas, and your spleen. Think about your lungs and the space that they take up in your body. The back of the lungs goes almost to your waist. And the top of the lungs goes up to your clavicle bones. As you breathe in, visualize that your rib cage is moving out to each side. As your rib cage moves out, the sternum or the bone above your heart gets wider. Your heart opens as you open your rib cage.

Relax your heart. Think of how many times it beats each minute. Tell it to slow down and rest. Also give it thanks.

Go to the base of your spine and slowly walk up your spine with your attention, relaxing each vertebra as you move up. Visualize your vertebrae and move each vertebra slightly so that there is more space between each one. Feel your spine growing longer. Feel your legs growing longer, and feel your arms growing longer. The top of your head is moving up.

Visualize the place on your spine where your cranium sits; psychically open a little space there.

Relax the back of your head, the top of your head. Relax both ears. Feel your ear lobes growing longer. Relax your eyes. Imagine that your eyes are two heavy marbles that are falling to the back of your head. Relax your cheek bones. Unlock your jaw. Relax your tongue. Relax your nose. Feel that it is becoming flat and moving into your face. Feel that your face is becoming flatter and rounder.

Feel that your whole body is relaxed and that you are getting warmer and heavier. See an orange color in your right shoulder and have it move down your body. See a green color on your left shoulder and have it move down your body.

Feel your whole body relaxed. Your body is heavy, relaxed and warm.

Closing-Up Script

Either one of these scripts can be used at the end of any imagery session.

Now see yourself at home. It is evening and everyone else is asleep. There is no work to be done. Everything can wait until tomorrow. You are in your favorite chair in the house. You are feeling a little drowsy and warm. You curl up a little and cover yourself, if it feels right. You are feeling content and at peace and in your heart you feel love for yourself.

Or

You find yourself at a warm body of water. It is not too hot or too cold. The temperature of the air and water are just right for you. Somehow you are lying on a gigantic leaf out in the water. You feel very safe and secure on the leaf. The water is rocking the leaf gently and you feel your body moving up and down, being rocked. You feel warm and your body is extended. You stretch out. Your whole body is extended and warm. The air becomes a little cooler, and you curl up. As you do that gigantic petals fold around you. They are alabaster color and scented. You feel nurtured and safe.

Imagery Script One: Power Animal

(Do the *Relaxation Script* first.)

You are outside in a place where you have been many times before. Every time you have gone there you have felt good about the place and also content about yourself. You start noticing details about where you are: the color of the dirt, the shape, form, texture, and smell of the plants around you. What colors stand out the most? What textures attract you? You notice the color of the sky and whether or not there are any clouds. You notice smells or sounds. Does the wind make a noise? Do you feel the wind on your cheek? You start walking, and notice how your foot feels when it moves, and whether or not you make a noise as you walk. Your hand brushes against a plant, a bush, or a tree. You notice how that feels.

You are walking along, and you feel happy and good about yourself. There are things to do, but you don't have to worry about them today.

Soon you find a spot to sit down and rest awhile. It may be a little clearing. [Sometimes people are on boats so you may want to make modifications to include that possibility.] You notice a movement over to the side, and you have a sense that an animal is coming to see you. It may be a wild animal or an imaginary animal, but you are not afraid. You know that the animal means you no harm.

The animal starts coming toward you. You notice details about the animal's fur or feathers. You notice textures and colors. The animal comes up to you.

Now let your imagery roll. See what happens with the animal. Does it talk to you? Do you touch it? Does it have a gift for you? It may take you somewhere, or the two of you may simply stare at each other. [Pause for at least a minute or two. Sometimes I get anxious when leading imagery and want to rush things. I count in my head or watch a second hand to make sure I am giving people time to let their imagery move.]

Now have your imagery with your animal complete itself. [Pause.] After it is complete, let that imagery fade. But don't let the sense that you had when you looked at the animal fade. What kind of feeling did you have when you were with the animal?

[Do the *Closing-Up Script* now.]

[Debrief.]

Imagery Script Two: A Loved One

This script was initially developed as an exercise to teach participants to "focus in" on an image. Many times, participants will see a vague form or a color without a form. By focusing in, or learning to look with the mind's eye in a concentrated and direct way, participants will be able to create vivid imagery over time. It was a surprise that this imagery exercise turned into much more than practice in creating vivid imagery. By focusing in on a loved one, participants opened their hearts and were moved in very deep ways. They felt an enormous amount of love from their loved ones during this exercise. It works well to do this exercise with partners and have participants take turns imaging. While partner A is imaging, partner B asks questions to help A focus in on the image. A tells B what he or she sees in as much detail as possible.

[Relaxation Script]

I want you to think about someone you love. Possibly see the people you love very much in your mind's eye. See each person one by one, and then choose one person to work with in this imagery session. The main emotion to be addressed is love. Therefore, if anger or other strong emotions come up when you see a loved one, do not pick that person.

Now let the person you have chosen come into your imagery field. The purpose of this exercise is to focus on some detail about the way this person looks.

First see the person at some distance, then start looking at the person with great concentration. As you keep looking at the person, some aspect about this person will come into focus. It may be the pores on the person's cheek, or it may be the texture of the hair. As you focus on a perceptual detail about the person, keep looking, keep looking.

Now notice what you see in great detail.

[Leave at least a two minute pause here.]

Pay attention to what is happening in your heart as you image the detail about this person. Notice how your stomach or other areas in your body feels.

Slowly let the image fade, but keep the feeling in your heart. Come back slowly to this time and space.

[Closing-Up Script.]

[Debrief.]

Imagery Script Three: Inner Child

[Relaxation Script.]

You find yourself outside standing at the opening of a meadow. It is a wide meadow, with many trees around it. There is tall grass around the perimeter near the trees, and there could be some wild flowers amidst the grass. You notice smells and colors. You notice the different colors of greens in the trees and the grasses. You also look at the trunks of the trees and notice the texture and color of the trunks.

Over to one side of the meadow there is a child playing. There is something familiar about the child. The child may be playing on a swing set, climbing, sitting alone, singing, or playing with stones. The child could be doing anything; you fill in the picture.

You start moving closer to the child and you notice more and more familiar things. Soon you realize that it is you as a child. You are watching your child self. You notice what the child is wearing, how the child looks, and what the child is doing. At first the child does not notice you. You are standing and watching.

After a time, the child looks at you. You approach the child and see what kind of interaction will ensue. Make sure that you let the child be the lead in this interaction or dialogue. Does the child talk to you, or do you talk to the child? Does the child want you to do something or want you to say something? Do you want to say something to the child? Notice the child's facial expression and body language. [Give participants at least two minutes here to let the imagery spring from the deep self in the unconscious.]

Now let the imagery complete itself. Is there anything you want to say to your child self before you go? Before you leave your child self, you must put her or him in a place of safety until you come back to talk and interact again. You can put your child self in a room where he or she has always felt safe. You can put your child self in your heart, or in any other special place. Make sure that the child feels safe before you leave her or him.

As you say goodbye to your child self pay attention to the feelings in your body and your sense of your relationship to your child. There may be more work to do with your child, but put him or her in a place of safety now. You can come back and do more work another time.

When you're ready, come back to this place and time.

[Closing-Up Script.]

[Debrief.]

Imagery Script Four: Mythic Journey Script

[Relaxation Script.]

You find yourself in your bedroom. It could be any room that you have ever had as a bedroom. And it could be an imaginary room that you like and would feel happy in. You start looking around your room, and you notice things. Is there a dresser or another piece of furniture in the room? Notice the color and surface of that piece of furniture. What else do you notice as you look around the room? What colors and textures are there? What objects do you see that remind you of your family or past events?

You know you are about to take a journey, so you start making preparations. You may want to have your child self join you. If so, the child self appears in the room. You look in the closet, and you find capes for both of you to put on. Notice the color of the cape. You also may want to put a hat on both of you. Or give both of you a shield, sword, necklace, or special amulet. Take your time in deciding what to put on. You want to feel strong and empowered on this journey.

Soon you are ready to go. You open the bedroom door, go to the front door and open that too. But instead of what you might usually see when you open the door, you see a woods in front of you. It is beautiful. There are trees, bushes, and many shades of green. There may be birds singing or flowers blooming. The sky is blue. You start your journey into the woods, for you know you are bound for a special destination. You hear the noise of an animal nearby, and you realize that your power animal has come to be with you. The three of you, child, adult, and animal proceed into the woods.

As you move into the woods, you notice sounds, textures, movements, and colors. You may reach out and touch something. You also notice how your body feels as you move.

After a bit, you notice that the trees are becoming thicker and the greens are darker. You can see less of the sky because of the thick branches overhead. You can smell the dirt more, the foliage is darker and moister.

As you move further into the dense forest, you realize that you will soon be approaching a cave. This is your destination. You are approaching the entrance to the cave. You need to assess whether or not you want to go into the cave. You may want to confer with your animal and child self.

If you decide to go in, you proceed into the entrance of the cave. Somehow you can see in the cave and can notice the details of the rock. You may even see precious metals, gems, or crystals. You move down into the cave, going deeper into the Earth.

You proceed down quite a ways and see ahead of you a chamber-like room. You have a sense that there is something in that room for you. You move into the room and then let your imagery move of its own accord. [Give participants time here. You may want to offer a few suggestions about what they might see, depending on what your intuition is telling you. When I have led this imagery, I almost always bring them back too soon, so make sure you give them time.]

Now it is time to start the journey back. If you found something in the cave, make sure that you bring it back with you, or give it to your child self. Start coming back. You can come back in any way that you like. You can come out of the cave the way you went in, and then move back through the dark forest and the green forest to the house. Alternatively, you could move by magic to the front of the house. Before you come back to this time and place, make sure you put your animal and child self in safe places. Your animal can stay in this woods or another woods, and your child self can go to a safe room and/or come forward by being placed in your heart. As you are putting your animal and child self in safe places, keep a fix on what you brought back from the cave.

[Closing-Up Script.]

[Debrief.]

Imagery Script Five: Resolution with Family Figures

This seems to be a significant imagery exercise to do because so much energy is blocked in the unconscious due to unresolved conflicts and issues with family members, either current family or family of origins. It is difficult, however, to write a script to do this, because the family member involved, and the type of issue, varies for each person. In general, though, rage from a pain inflicted or the lack of acceptance are the most general repressed emotions. On the spiritual path it is necessary to release these emotions when the person is ready. Of course, participants should not be pushed to do this imagery. An imagery leader can give a group or an individual the choice of doing this imagery, or the leader can be observant during imagery debriefings to see if family figures are coming up in imagery exercises.

The general idea is to get the person in a safe setting where the person feels empowered. If the event with the family happened when the person was a child, it is good to have the child there, but in a place of safety behind the adult self. Any symbols of power that can be given to the person are positive. The leader can suggest symbols, but they should only be used if they feel correct to the person. Sometimes it is good to have the family relative shrunk in size, as well, if the relative is threatening to the participant. The basic plan is the get the person to act out rage, pain, or sadness in the imagery. The imagery needs to be continued until it feels complete to the person. It could be that the release of some of these emotions will take many years. "Completing" a session, then, does not mean solving the issue, it just means complete at that time. *Keep the person safe in the image. If the person becomes scared or anxious, create more distance between the person and the relative.* If there is no way of making the person feel safe in the imagery, put the relative in a place where they cannot bother the person (i.e., an island, a house in the mountains, etc.) until the person is ready to try to work with the relative again. This script is sketchier than others, since many things would need to be individualized. The imagery leader should add more detail and flesh it out to make it fit the situation. You may want to have the participants talk about the relative to a partner before this imagery to open the situation up.

[Relaxation Script.]

Create a setting in your imagery that feels good to you. Find a place that will be safe for you. It could be outside, a room, or a gym. You choose the one. [Give specific suggestions. Leave a long pause. Check to see that the person is comfortable.]

After you find the setting that is safe, notice details in the setting. Move around in the setting. Bring in anything that you would like—animal, child self, symbols of power.

Now bring in the family member in question. Place this person far enough away from you that you feel safe. Also if it helps, you may want to shrink this relative in size, or put the relative in a cage, or behind a lucite wall.

Now say what you need to say to the person. This is your imagination, so anything can happen. What happens in the imagery will not hurt the person. The idea is for you to move what belongs to your relative out of your aura back to his or her aura. You can hit the family member in the image, poke it, yell at it, whatever seems to come out of you. [Give quite a bit of time here.]

Continue this until it is complete. If you cannot talk to the person, bring someone else in who can express your feelings.

Complete this imagery, by putting the family member some place where he or she will not be able to bother you. You don't have to express everything this time. You can bring this family member out when you feel ready to express more. Notice where in your body you are feeling something. Is it warm, hard, dense, or agitated? Now come back to this time and place.

[Closing-Up Script.]

[Debrief. Debriefing is essential in this type of exercise.*]*

Other Imagery Scene Ideas

Stress Reduction:

Outside setting with a person the participant loves.

Inner Strength:

A water setting; the individual dives in and brings back something from the deep.

Idealized self image; individuals see themselves as they would like to be.

Individual goes to a cave, sees an elder, and asks a question.

Emotional Strength:

A person goes to a house and sees an old person. It is the person's elder self.

A person is relaxed and then a scene that the person fears is introduced. The fear is exaggerated to show that the person will be okay, even if the thing that is feared happens.

Early recollections; a person goes to the home when he or she was small. The person notices who is in the house and how the person feels about each one.

Decision Making and Goal Setting:

A person images what the outcome will be of certain choices.

A person sees him or herself reaching a goal.

Learning:

A student watches the hand as it writes material that is to be memorized.

A student sees himself or herself in a previous learning setting when he or she succeeded.

A student visualizes the problem to be solved and waits for a solution.

A student visualizes characters or events from a book before writing about them.

A student visualizes to music before doing an art project or writing poetry or fiction.

Physical Healing:

A pain is found in the body. The person images how big the pain is, how much space it takes up, what color it is, and what its textures look like. The person gives permission to the deep self to transform the image of the pain, to heal the pain, and to complete the healing process.

Bibliography

Achterberg, J. *Imagery in Healing: Shamanism and Modern Medicine.* Boston: Shambhala, 1985.

Ahsen, A. (1982). "Imagery in Perceptual Learning and Clinical Application." *Journal of Mental Imagery* 6: 157-186

Andrews, L. *Medicine Woman.* New York: HarperCollins, 1981.

Basmahian, J., ed. *Biofeedback Principles and Practice for Clinicians.* Baltimore, MD: Williams & Wilkins, 1989.

Benally, H. (1988). "Diné Philosophy of Learning." *Journal of Navajo Education* 6: 9-13.

Bohm, D. *Wholeness and the Implicate Order.* London & Boston: Routledge & Kegan Paul, 1980.

Bower, B. (1986). "Million Cell Memories." *Science News* 130: 313-315.

Brown, G. W. and J. S. Wolf. (1986). "Development of Intuition in the Gifted." *Journal for the Education of the Gifted* 9: 157-164

Campbell, Joseph. *The Hero with a Thousand Faces.* Princeton, NJ: Princeton University Press, 1972.

Cerney, M. S. *Psychotherapy and the Remorseful Patient.* Binghamton, NY: Haworth Press, 1989.

Cousins, N. *Anatomy of an Illness as Perceived by the Patient: Reflections on Healing and Regeneration.* New York: Norton, 1979.

Dalai Lama Tsong-ka-pa, and J. Hopkins. *Tantra in Tibet.* Ithaca, NY: Snow Lion, 1977.

Eliade, M. *Shamanism: Archaic Techniques of Ecstasy.* Princeton, NJ: Princeton University Press, 1972.

Farah, M. J. (1984). "The Neurological Basis of Mental Imagery: A Componential Analysis." *Cognition* 2: 55-76.

Fromme, D. K. and J. Daniel (1984). "Neurolinguistic Programming Examined: Imagery, Sensory Mode and Communication." *Journal of Counseling Psychology* 31: 387-390.

Gallegos, E. S. (1983). "Animal Imagery, the Chakra System and Psychotherapy." *Journal of Transpersonal Psychology* 15, (2): 125-136.

Giesler, P. V. (1984). "Batcheldorian Psychodynamics in the Umbanda Ritual Trance Consultation." *Parapsychology Review* (November/December), 5-9.

Goldstein, L. (1984). "A Reconsideration of Right Hemispheric Activity During Visual Imagery, REM Sleep, and Depression." *Research Communications in Psychology, Psychiatry and Behavior* 9: 139-148.

Halifax, J. *Shamanic Voices: A Survey of Visionary Narratives.* New York.: E.P. Dutton, 1979.

Hall, S. S. (1989). "A Molecular Code Links Emotions, Mind and Health." *Smithsonian* (June), 62-71.

Hari Das, Baba. *Silence Speaks: From the Chalkboard of Baba Hari Das.* Santa Cruz, CA: Sri Rama Foundation, 1977.

Harner, M. *The Way of the Shaman.* New York: Bantam Books, 1982.

Hebb, D. O. (1968). "Concerning Imagery." *Psychological Review* 75: 466-477.

Houston, J. *The Search for the Beloved: Journeys in Sacred Psychology.* Los Angeles: Jeremy P. Tarcher, 1987.

Jordan, C. S. (1984). "Psychophysiology of Structural Imagery in Post-Traumatic Stress Disorders." *Journal of Mental Imagery* 8: 51-66.

Jung, C. *Analytical Psychology.* New York: Moffat, Yard, 1916.
———. *The Archetypes and the Collective Unconscious,* 2nd Edition. Princeton, NJ: Princeton University Press, 1968.

Lashley, C.K. *Brain Mechanisms and Intelligence: A Quantitative Study of Injury to the Brain.* Chicago: University of Chicago Press, 1929.

Lozanov, G. *Suggestology and Outlines of Suggestopedy.* New York: Gordon & Breach, 1978.

Maslow, A. H. *Motivation and Personality.* 2nd Edition. New York: Harper & Row, 1970.

Masui, T. "The Patient's Efforts and Psychotherapy: The Images of Symptoms." Presented at the 3rd International Conference, Fukuoka, Japan, 1987.

Murdock, M. *Spinning Inward: Using Guided Imagery for Children for Learning, Creativity and Relaxation.* Boston and London: Shambhala, 1987.

Nelson, A. *How to Focus the Distractible Child.* Saratoga, CA: R & E Publishers, 1984.

———. (1988). "Imagery's Physiological Base: The Limbic System, a Review Paper. *Journal of the Society for Accelerative Learning and Teaching* 13: 363-373.

Nideffer, R. M. *Athlete's Guide to Mental Training.* Champaign, IL: Human Kinetics, 1985.

Perls, F. S. *Gestalt Therapy Verbatim.* Ed. John Stevens. Lafayette, CA: Real People Press, 1969.

Pribram, K.H. *Language of the Brain: Experimental Paradoxes and Principles in Neuropsychology.* New York: Brandon House, 1981.

Pylyshyn, Z. (1981). "The Imagery Debate: Analogue Media Versus Tacit Knowledge." *Psychological Review* 88: 16-45.

Ram Dass, *Be Here Now.* Boulder, CO: Hanuman Foundation, 1971.

———. *The Only Dance There Is.* New York: J. Aranson, 1976.

Swami Rama, R. Ballentine, and S. Ajaya, *Yoga and Psychotherapy: The Evolution of Consciousness.* Honesdale, PA: Himalayan International Institute, 1976.

Rider, M. S., J. W. Floyd, and J. Kirkpatrick. (1985). "The Effect of Music, Imagery and Relaxation on Adrenal Corticosteroids and the Re-entrainment of Circadian Rhythms." *Journal of Music Therapy* 12: 46-58.

Roberts, J. *Seth Speaks: The Eternal Validity of the Soul.* New York: Prentice Hall Press, 1972.

Rogers, C. *Freedom to Learn.* New York: C. E. Merrill, 1969.

———. *On Becoming a Person: A Therapist's View of Psychotherapy.* Boston: Houghton Mifflin, 1961.

Rossman, M. *Healing Yourself: A Step-by-Step Program for Better Health Through Imagery.* New York: Pocket Books, 1987.

Ryan, E. B., G. W. Ledger, and K. A. Weed (1987). "Acquisition and Transfer of an Integrative Imagery Strategy by Young Children." *Child Development* 58: 443-452.

Sheikh, A. A. *Imagery: Current Theory, Research and Applications.* New York: John Wiley, 1983.

Sheikh A. A. and K. S. Sheikh. *Imagery in Education: Imagery in Education Processes.* Farmingdale, NY: Baywood Publishing Company, 1985

Shorr, J. E., G. E. Sobel, P. Robin, and J. A. Connella. *Imagery: Its Many Dimensions and Applications.* New York: Plenum Press, 1979.

Springer, S. P. and G. Deutsch, *Left Brain, Right Brain.* San Francisco: W.H. Freeman, 1981.

Storm, H. *Seven Arrows.* New York: HarperCollins, 1987.

Stutley, M. and J. Stutley. *Dictionary of Hinduism: Its Mythology, Folklore and Development.* London: Routledge, 1977.

Sundar, *Space Channeling.* Santa Cruz, CA: Rainbow Bridge Construction, 1976.

Twining, W. E. (1949). "Mental Practice and Physical Practice in Learning a Motor Skill." *Research Quarterly* 20: 432-435.

VanKrevelen, A. (1983). "Evoking Creative Imagery in Children Using Guided Fantasy." *Academic Psychology Bulletin* 5: 85-87.

Weschler, B. (1987). "A New Prescription: Mind Over Malady." *Discovery* (February), 51-61.

West, M. *The Psychology of Meditation*. Atlanta, GA: Clarendon Press, 1987.

Wilber, K. (1989). "For a Star Dakini." *Common Boundary* (May/June), 10, 11.

———. *Up From Eden: A Transpersonal View of Human Evolution*. Garden City, NY: Anchor Press/Doubleday, 1981.

Wilber, K., ed. The Holographic Paradigm and Other Paradoxes. Boston: Shambhala, 1987.

Ywahoo, D. *Voices of Our Ancestors* Boston: Shambhala, 1987.

Index

A

acceptance, 74
Achterberg, J. 48, 150
Adey, W. R., 143
affirmations, 61, 101
after-life experience, 90
ahankar, 23, 24
aligning to Earth, 17
Amygdala, 46
anger, 65
animal nature, 68
arcana, major, 96
arcana, minor, 96
archetype, martyr, 10
asanas, 24
atman, 8, 25, 27, 47
attachment, 61, 115
aura, 91, 108
aura reading, 97
automatic writing, 85

B

Begay, D. 14
Benally, H. 14
beyond dualism, 10

bliss, 119
bodywork therapies, 30
Bohm, D. 22
brain, 141
   paleomonalian 144
Buddha, 57, 60
buddhi, 24, 25
Buddhism, 115
Buddhist worldview, 113
butterfly, 31

C

Campbell, J. 67, 109, 114
chakras, 80
channeling, 85, 95
chemical experiment, 23
Cherokee, 9
child image, 53, 122
chittas, 23, 24, 57, 107, 120
choice, 73
closing up script, 160
codependence, 110
cognitive process, 42
collective unconscious, 21, 47
Connie's anger, 101

conscious mind, 5, 7, 9, 20, 23, 24, 29, 39, 43, 46, 47, 71, 73, 74
consciousness, 115
control, 92
cortex, 46, 47
Cousins, N., 149
coyote, 1
creative force, 48
creativity, 43

D

Dalai Lama, 116
darshan, 85
death, 114
decision making, 173
demons, 103
denial, 72
detachment, 30, 60
Deutch, G. 147
Deva Lama, 86
Diné wheel, 14
disequilibrium, 76
disintegration, 75
drugs, hallucinatory, 106
drumming, 25
dualism, 4, 5, 6, 7, 9, 88
dying to ego, 59

E

ecstatic experience, 47
ego, 24, 92
    controlling, 60
    death, 59

Eliade, M. 104
emotional strength, 173
emotional work, 71
emotions, 58, 66, 67, 69, 77, 91
    transorming, 81
energy levels, 87
enlightenment, 121, 124
ethnobotany, 8
evolution of consciousness, 109

F

Farah, M., 147
Fuller, B., 85

G

Gawain, S., 101
goal setting, 173

H

Halifax, J., 105
Harner, M., 105
healing, 8, 46, 47, 66, 174
health, psychological, 24
hero-heroine, 109
Hindu reality, 23
hippocampus, 46, 47
Holy Spirit, 48
Hopi migration stories, 3
Houston, J., 75
humility, 78

I

I Ching, 95
Iitoi, 11
imagery, 37, 38, 41, 42, 45, 46,
    47, 98, 141, 143, 145, 148,
    150
    exercise, 17, 31, 33, 53, 98,
    117, 124
    how to lead others, 51
    scripts, 153, 156, 161, 163,
    167, 170, 173
    story, 34, 55, 83, 101, 118
    work, 47
indigenous people, 8
inner child, 165
inner strength, 173
intent, 73
intuition, 19, 20, 21, 28, 29, 67,
    86, 92
intuitive mind, 20

J

Jill, 83
Jordan, C., 46

K

Kabbalah, 96
Kali, Goddess, 75
karma, 50, 71, 78, 93, 108
karmic debris, 107
kinesthesia, 42
Krishna, 90

Krishnamurti, 22
kundalini energy, 81

L

Lashley, C., 142
left brain model, 11, 145, 146
limbic system, 9, 10, 46, 47,
    143, 144, 145
loved one script, 163
Lozanov, G., 45

M

manas, 23
manifestations, 61
Mark, 34
Maslow, A. 25, 60, 64
Maslow's self-actualizing ten-
    dency, 25
Masui, T., 66
material world, 120
maya, 120
meditation, 24, 25, 29, 72, 101
memory, 23, 24, 44, 47
metaphoric thinking, 14
metaphors, 66
middle brain, 9
mind, 28
    -body connection, 46
    quieting the, 29
    sensory motor, 23
    stuff, 107, 120
model of reality, 12

Monica's birth, 55
movement, 42
multiple realities, 15
music, 52
mythic journey, 167

N

Native American wheel, 3
Navajo tribe, 14
needs, hierarchy of, 64
neurons, 141
non-dualistic reality model, 88

O

O'odham maze, 11
oracles, 95, 97

P

pain, 60, 65
    transforming, 33
Pangaea, 1, 2
peace, 119
Perls, F., 65
persona, 40
Pert, C., 148
physiology, 141
Plains Medicine Wheel, 12
power animal, 98, 161
prana, 89
pranamaya, 89
prayer, 28, 29

predetermined goal, 153
Pribram, K., 67, 141, 144, 148
priestcraft, 9
psyche, 37
psychic awareness, 94, 98
psychic duals, 111
psychic energy surges, 123
psychic murky zones, 88
paychic perception, 86, 91, 92
psychic work, 91
psychoneuroimmunology, 148
Pylyshyn, Z. 48, 49

R

Ram Dass, 73, 74, 106
reiki, 30
relationships, 127
relaxation, 31, 157
relaxation instructions, 154
resolution with family figures, 170
rhythm, 47, 52
Rider, M., 45
right brain model, 11, 145, 146
rituals, 8
Rogers, C., 60, 66
rolfing, 30
Ruff, M., 148

S

self
    deep, 27, 30, 48, 74
    higher, 48
    real, 25

sense of stability, 23
serpent, 7, 8, 81, 103
sexuality, 79
shakes, 123
shamanism, Tibetan, 116
shamans, 47, 69, 98, 104, 109, 111
Sikh religion, 81
smell, 42
songs, 8
spirit healers, 47
spirit self, 8
spiritual body, 64, 76, 81
spiritual journey, 123
spiritual path, 12, 58, 128
spiritaul practice, 41
sports, 46
Springer, S., 147
stress reduction, 173
subtleness, 79
suggestology, 45
superlearning, 44
symbol, 153
synchronicity, 79

T

taking flight, 124
Tantric Buddhism, 116
Tao, 113
    circle of, 77
Taoism, 77
tarot, 96
taste, 42
Teresa, Mother, 75
terror, 103
thought forms, 5

Tohono O'odham tribe, 11
touch
transcendence, 116
transformation, 116
trauma, 46
    childhood, 75
Tsalgi tribe, 9
Twining, W., 46

U

unconscious, 7
unconscious mind, 7, 8, 15, 20, 29, 71
underworld, 104
uniting with the Earth's core, 117

V

vision quests, 8
visualization, 42, 43
void, 113
vultures and eagles, 118

W

Wagenen, W. Van, 145
Wawgiwulk, 11
West, M., 47
Western society, 2
Western world view, 3
wheel metaphor, 10
wheel models, 11
Wilbur, K., 24, 59, 87, 127

wild human animal, 68
wildman archetype, 22
wisdom, 24, 25
wounds, 49

Y

yoga, 24, 29, 72, 89
   Hatha, 30
   postures, 24
   teacher, 123

Annabelle Nelson has a Ph. D. in Developmental and Child Psychology, an M. S. in Special Education, and a B. A. in Psychology and Mathematics from the University of Kansas. She is a researcher, author, curriculum developer, and has taught children, teenagers, and adults. With a lifelong love for imagery and the spiritual path, her interests range from learning-theory to mysticism. She presently works in private practice with people who want to integrate spiritual concepts into daily life.

Annabelle Nelson is also the author of *Curriculum Design Techniques* (W. C. Brown Publishers) *How to Focus the Distractable Child* (R & E Publications), and *The Learning Wheel: Multicultural and Holistic Lesson Planning* (due to be published in Spring 1994 by Zephyr).